T0070169

In Pursuit of an Entrepreneurial Culture

RAUSHAN GROSS

authorHOUSE®

AuthorHouse™
1663 Liberty Drive
Bloomington, IN 47403
www.authorhouse.com
Phone: 833-262-8899

Published by AuthorHouse 08/02/2022

ISBN: 978-1-6655-6731-2 (sc)
ISBN: 978-1-6655-6732-9 (e)

To my wife, Melinda, and our beautiful and intelligent children, Harrison and Harper. And to my students who play such a large part in this journey.

Contents

Introduction

The world is ever changing, which we all know so well. But in many ways, there is a conception of the world as being stationary. A stationary world does not account for major or minor changes, adjustments, or a pursuit of the highest level of economic growth. A stationary mindset implies an economy that does not grow and that is without self-generating pockets for creative people to act as creators. Here we trace a clear but abstract economic pattern. There is a marketplace pattern. The pattern is best described as relentless pursuits by entrepreneurs who address the old and figure out the new. Newness and economic development abound throughout history. History is one of the greatest economic analytical tools, as it reports the transition effects of a changing economy, resources, migrations, cultural amalgamation, and the genius that resulted in one state of living to a better state of living via entrepreneurs' relentless pursuits of market opportunity and a better way of doing things.

Not all that glitters is gold. I do not purport that all forms of entrepreneurship are in the best interests of humanity, nor are all entrepreneurs ethical. For sure, in the past, some entrepreneurs have conducted themselves in unethical ways.

Ethical entrepreneurial conduct, while important in how society holds sacred values and customs that are conducive to morality, nevertheless is not the immediate aim of this book. With most things, one bad apple cannot spoil the bunch. This book seeks to capture the meaning and nature of personal experience as an individual entrepreneur, and of society at large partaking in the entrepreneurial function of a marketplace. Each person, as part of the larger whole, exercises subjectivity—a brand of subjectivity that refers to how the "inner conscious life of the human persons, while maintaining an inner life, remain open to the world around them." [1]

Along with ethics is the notion that with freedom comes responsibility. Freedom and an ethical culture of entrepreneurship is peaceful entrepreneurship; in this sense, entrepreneurship as an act in the marketplace using tools and knowledge. This knowledge has accumulated in human society because of the experiences of civilization and the explicit knowledge that has been "passed down on to successive generations embody on the results of experience without the whole of the experience being transmitted." [2] Simply put, you, me, and everyone else are entrepreneurs with various consequential effects as to our impact on investments and use of resources, but the act itself has been handed down through means of culture as an accumulated

[1] . A. J. Santelli, J. Sikkenga, R. A. Sirico, S. Yates, and G. Zúñiga, *The Free Person and the Free Economy: A Personalist View of Market Economics* (Lanham, MD: Lexington Books, 2002).

[2] . A. Kemp, *Essays on Individuality* (Indianapolis, IN: Liberty Press, 1977).

stock of knowledge from generations past, much of which is least understood.

What is the entrepreneur without the accumulated store of knowledge on how to use resources, understanding of the transmission of knowledge via prices, and skill to enter markets both far and near? In fact, knowledge of and discovery of entrepreneurial opportunities are thus apparent because of the use of information and the application of knowledge pertaining to a market that one does not have to obtain on one's own. The discovery process is unarticulated and, in many cases, unintelligible to the nonactor. But real people, on the other hand, need a different kind of knowledge, something akin to a process or a ritual that works as a guidepost to know what is profitable and what is not, what is going to serve someone else or not. Real people seek to use the available knowledge of others to increase their efforts in entrepreneurial pursuits.

This book explores the contrary stationary and unchanging conception of the world. In fact, what is highlighted and much needed is to show the relentless pursuit of a culture of a constantly changing world. The catalyst of a less static world via a market economy is entrepreneurship and the entrepreneurs who are consistently moving toward growth. Unlike many books on entrepreneurship, this book views entrepreneurship as a force propagated by you and me. In a broad sense, we are all entrepreneurs and are affected by the market function of entrepreneurship. However, there are long-run and short-run stabilities and instabilities created by the ebb and flow of entrepreneurial activity. This is well-known and tends to be factual according to historical accounts. Certainly, entrepreneurs can create from a heterogeneous stock of personal resources, but the opportunity and the ability to grasp a discovery can have the allure of a *creatio ex nihilo*—creation out of nothing.

Further, the action that underpins entrepreneurship is to a large extent a creative endeavor because it is the inarticulate mandate toward the discovery process. In other words, the creativity that goes into the inarticulate *rules* involved in the discovery of profitable opportunity is by its very nature impregnated in the production of the discovery process itself. Glückel of Hameln said it best in describing the entrepreneurial creative process: "He can make much out of little, how Judah Berlin with a capital as good as nothing achieved great wealth and so become a great man." [3] Glückel of Hameln's point is that the creative aspect of entrepreneurship has been as persistent today as it has during the fifteenth century experienced by Glückel centuries ago. In the context of entrepreneurship, an age-old tradition, therefore, is the creation of something from nothing. It is real people creating better lives via the formation of capital, finding an inarticulate discovery brought about by productive purposes, and thereby, serving themselves and others, sometimes as if from nothing to something.

However, these short-run and long-run changes in techniques, inventions, and healthy investments overshadow the adverse effects and pitfalls of malinvestments on the part of entrepreneurs. Changes occur, as few things are fixed. This notion can be drawn out through a historical analysis. However, the idea is that people have goals and

---

[3] . R. C. Schiller, *Glückel of Hameln. The Memoirs of Glückel of Hameln*, trans. M. Lowenthal (New York, NY: Shocken Books, 1977).

plans, and those goals and plans change, and those changes affect other people directly or indirectly. Any change in circumstances forces individuals to either act or not to act. Future development is influenced by previous development. The fact of the following assertions is predicated on the persistence of a culture that rewards actors to assume risk; actors in the marketplace respond to market forces because market forces are ever changing. A culture such as an entrepreneurial one encompasses changes to language, money, demand, supply, consumer preferences, value scales, prices, marketing, and technology. The entrepreneurial culture is social practices—visible and invisible—human interaction conveyed in language, laws, customs, knowledge, and capabilities in the market economy. Humans socially interacting using intelligence is "the expression of man's response to the changing problems set by the environment and by his fellow men ... For meeting any new situation, new thoughts, new aptitudes, new action will be required." [4]

Entrepreneurs always act in response to current conditions to obtain prospects that are future oriented. Action is a human condition where one's actions are pointed to a future state rather than a past state. Action in the human form is directed toward a better state or condition than the individual was in previously. Such action looks the same as non-entrepreneurial action. So, what distinguishes the two action progenitors? The entrepreneurial action discovers in a marketplace a way of employing heterogeneous capital resources with the complement of labor to enter markets

---

[4] . M. C. Cipolla, *Guns, Sails, and Empires: Technological Innovation and the Early Phases of European Expansion, 1400–1700* (Manhattan, KS: Sunflower University Press, 1965).

before competitors. They act with haste to make a better situation for themselves with the best use of their resources. In all regards, the resources are finite, including time. Entrepreneurs take initiative, are independent thinkers, and consistently seek to better their situations; Aristotle would have called them prime movers. How entrepreneurs think of and use time is different from non-entrepreneurs, which, in any event, would give them this formative name: entrepreneur. Entrepreneurs have shown a relentless pursuit of innovation and skills that, when realized and manifested into a service or products, has changed the course of technological advances, such as advances in consumer goods, manufacturing goods, and technology in weapons and artillery that have made winners and losers of vast empires.

This book introduces a narrower cultural viewpoint of entrepreneurship that holistically encapsulates individual knowledge, market processes, innovative use of resources, and the creation of these factors used in the pursuit of entrepreneurial action. In this case, culture is not predicated on characteristics pertaining to the variation of the given world; rather, it is a collection of ideas and practices that cross over geographical regions more broadly. This definition of culture of entrepreneurship used throughout this book comprises known processes and opportunities and individuals' responses related to social processes that enable engagement in marketplace activity; cultural context does shape group patterns, but patterns are sometimes broken, readapted, changed, or modified to meet new circumstances or new challenges. In this book, the term *culture* is held in its strictest sense of the term, primarily focusing on values, attitudes, history, language, markets, communication, and a few heroes. I have narrowly defined culture as a learned set of behaviors and values that are aligned with conventions expressed through actions that have been consciously known or unknown to the individual but are known by the greater actions of those who practice in the particular institutions and abide by the real or perceived rules of the institutions set by a cultural framework. Cultures are not static institutions; they can be transmitted.

What makes this book important is that within a cultural group is how we see, perceive, and realize that there are market opportunities that have gone unnoticed or, in some cases, do not exist. The entrepreneur's subjective valuation of time and the use of time for future improvement signify they prioritize time. The entrepreneur wants to act sooner than later on profit opportunities. There is a difference between the consumer's time preference and the entrepreneur's time preference, and the subjective marginal utility of future and present pursuits and investments. Why do entrepreneurs view time differently than non-entrepreneurs? What is it about time that works positively toward the systemic process of discovery, development, and judgments needed to bring products to market? Better yet, what is the consequence of having a lower time preference toward effective market demand? Time preference in human action leads to the question of whether entrepreneurs enjoy short-run opportunities or profitable long-term opportunities (i.e., high or low time preference). Entrepreneurs have a time preference in which they create a firm and provide a service or product, or both.

Conversely, consumers have a time preference in

that they demand a service and/or product to meet their ability to pursue specific goals. Put differently, each market participant—the buyer and seller, the entrepreneur, and the consumer—measures goods subjectively via the function of time. All seek to economize, as differences in value are precisely determined by what goods are available at a specific time. What one does at a particular point in time reveals one's preferences for a consumer good. An entrepreneur's time is spent producing or creating either a novel product or a mundane product or service. It seems that, in this case—in regard to the valuation of a good or service, the time, and the change in market dynamics over time—the entrepreneur is willing to forgo future profit opportunities for marketplace opportunities that are closer to their personal time preference. This leads us to the purpose of this book: to bring together multiple ideas and processes that inform entrepreneurship from a cultural and knowledge-focused perspective.

Many entrepreneurial individuals within a given culture receives information from externally abstract-derived sources, including those within and without culture relevancies both past and present. Whichever side of the debate one is on does not eliminate the claim that information and knowledge are critical to an entrepreneur's profit or loss, competitiveness, and the ability to gain market share in a marketplace economy. The question is, how effective are the transmissions of cultural knowledge when tied to market participation that is relevant in and used in another region other than which the cultural knowledge previously exists? The old saying, *it is not where you are from but where you are at*, is essential to the context of culture and knowledge. Knowledge obtained in various markets—past or present—is harnessed through the market mechanisms (price, resources, consumer markets, dissatisfaction, money, etc.) and provide the entrepreneur with means to perceive the wants and needs of market consumers abstractly. Means and ends are relevant to the individual and are embedded in the time and place of the entrepreneurial group. Individual analysis or cultural-level analysis have either (or both) expert and mundane knowledge. Too often, the caricature is the boasted mainstream ways of conducting business. In this case, mundane knowledge is average knowledge to do things. It does not take brilliance of any sort to open a lemonade stand to serve thirsty neighbors. The same idea holds for many things that can be accomplished in the market economy.

Historically, and as contemporary business shows us, successful entrepreneurial groups or classes pursue those activities that require readily accessible knowledge. An entrepreneurs' Knowledge, and of course the mundane type, rewards them for applying the best use toward the needs of others. There is a tendency to view knowledge as static. Knowledge is viewed as a continuous flow on the other end of the spectrum. Hayek expressed that knowledge is uneven and decentralized for the most effective use by the many. There is no given amount of knowledge dispersed among the many individuals in society. [5] Entrepreneurs, in most cases, use knowledge either passed down through familial lines or via some form of extracted experience. There is a tendency to view the cultural knowledge passed down

---

[5] . F. A. Hayek, "The Use of Knowledge in Society," *The American Economic Review* 35, no. 4 (1945): 519–530.

through an entrepreneur or entrepreneurially defined group in a linear direction—you receive the knowledge externally and assimilate it and apply it. The contrary is the case, thereby moving in the opposite direction. Knowledge gained externally is based on the marketplace one finds oneself in at a particular time and place. Not all marketplaces in which business owners find themselves are the same, despite the attainment of knowledge brought down through familial lines and past generations.

Individuals or groups of individuals associated with any number of cultures encounter a history attached to the meaning the culture decides to embrace over time. Some of this is engaged in an industry in one region or another but is hardly represented in the same industry. Although associated with various cultures, people tend to break inefficient patterns that no longer serve the needs of the ideas or attitudes that at one time or another were cultivated. While we are aware of the supply-and-demand side of entrepreneurial market opportunity, what is not clear are the cultural aspects that motivate one to pursue an opportunity within and between markets. Given that markets are altogether different across the globe—markets in Taiwan are different than those of the Midwestern United States—the same entrepreneur operates differently and simultaneously in various markets.

There is an increasing number of marketplace opportunities, especially for those seeking to use entrepreneurship and entrepreneurial tools to participate in the market process. Nowadays, the knowledge, tools, and technologies of entrepreneurship are accessible to the average person. Digital and e-commerce platforms are open to transact business via Poshmark, eBay, Amazon, Facebook Marketplace, and the like. If you own a smartphone or have access to the Web, the opportunity is at your fingertips. The application of entrepreneurial knowledge, as we know, is a process and an ever-changing aspect of life. Finding a consumer need or creating a market space is within one's grasp if one dares to be aware of unforeseen resources that could go toward a new, more productive use than sitting idle. If we say that resources are inherently scarce, then how do we know as a society what is the best future use or allocation of a resource if new ideas of how to use a scarce resource are not competition? The end value of competitive processes in marketplace discovery is that it is not deliberately aimed at but is unpredictable in its results.

In most cases, the entrepreneur and consumer are intimately bound up in the market process. The entrepreneurial process takes place within economic and social institutions. However, institutions and emerging technologies allow what I like to refer to as mundane entrepreneurial opportunities, using existing resources and applying tacit and expert knowledge to the opportunities that relate to the day-to-day use of consumer acquisition. The idea of the free market hinges on one's ability to participate using one's knowledge and personal resources advanced in the pursuit to serve others cooperatively and humanely. This book draws from a mundane point of view the very idea of how anyone can participate in the marketplace with both tacit and expert knowledge—and, of course, technology— and pursue the mundaneness of entrepreneurship.

Part 1

Who can predict the number of births or deaths that will occur during the current year? Who can foresee the increase or reduction in expenditures that can occur in families? And yet the rice of the farmer's product naturally depends upon these unforeseen circumstances, and consequently; he conducts the enterprise of his farm with uncertainty.

—Richard Cantillon (1755)

It seems that several definitions can be attributed to the entrepreneur's actions and the process of entrepreneurship that derives from discoveries in a world of unexpected changes. Changes in a market economy that evoke reformulations and a reevaluation of entrepreneurs' expectations are primarily due to individual interpretations of changes and individual responses that are related to actions originating from a culture of entrepreneurship. The phenomenon of entrepreneurship is viewed based on its causes and its effects. What are the causes and effects of the *entrepreneurial hand* or the emerging pursuit of an entrepreneurial culture? It does not seem as though the term *entrepreneurship* has the same or similar connotation in many respects and contexts in which the action takes place. I do not believe that any one individual, class, or group of people owns the word *entrepreneur*. The entrepreneur and the causes of entrepreneurship can be applied to all walks of life. So, in this regard, it affects real people composed of you, me, your neighbor, and everyone else. We are all, in levels of consequential effects, entrepreneurs—just the effects are varied.

To be sure, there should not be a prevailing narrative that characterizes entrepreneurship only under the auspices of personality but rather characterizes it as the conditions in a marketplace that enable individuals through incentives to engage in the entrepreneurial societal function. The question that should be asked is how a culture of entrepreneurship optimizes and the institutional framework enables the entrepreneurial reservoir to increase the propensity of an entrepreneurial culture. The presumption is that a culture of entrepreneurship is likely to tap into, release, and guide untapped potential by use of the entrepreneurial hand. What are the circumstances or arrangements in society that allow the entrepreneurial hand to work in time and place? One would be hard pressed to link a particular context of the entrepreneur to a particular set of circumstances, because the world we live in is unevenly distributed. Too often, however, the prevailing narrative of the entrepreneur is that of the millionaire tech start-up and other famous individuals in the media. But, again, parts of this book discover an alternative view of the culture of entrepreneurship. Therefore, this book describes how entrepreneurship is for everyone, and it describes how real people can assume the economic function of the entrepreneur. Everyone is an entrepreneur! There is a relentless culture of entrepreneurship that, on many levels, can be exercised by everyone. Furthermore, what are the market institutions that allow everyone to participate in this function?

There is a prevailing theme and narrative surrounding the word entrepreneurship. This book extends that narrative to include that entrepreneurship is and can be for anybody—for real people in the real world. An entrepreneurial culture grows out of the act of human cooperation. The acts of human interaction and cooperation are entrepreneurship which is serving others by implementing capital resources, time, and energy. In this book I explain that the demands placed on the entrepreneur are ever changing, thereby necessitating interpretation of what is next to be created, developed, or invested in with limited resources. Based on the interpretation of these market forces, one then acts on perceived expectations.

The first section of this book highlights a straightforward yet abstract economic market pattern—that real people in the real world are in relentless pursuit of entrepreneurship. This pursuit goes beyond supply and demand. This book in many ways reflects our world of unexpected change—this is where the real-world entrepreneur culture exists. While entrepreneurship is a function with real effects that are pursued by real people, underscored on this fact is a relentless culture based on formal and informal societal rules and mores and folklore. The following chapters explain the real-world need for spontaneous interactions via competition in the marketplace that produce available knowledge for consumers and entrepreneurs, entrepreneurial leadership, and choice of consumption. Furthermore, this book also mentions how new or existing entrepreneurs should drop their buckets where they are and invest in the resources in their possession to serve their economic home—not to mention the do-it-yourself (DIY) entrepreneurs who use the most contemporary e-platforms to participate in the market process by serving and innovating for consumers using their resources, skills, or money via transition-based e-platforms to reach the most remote consumer.

1

The Relentless Benefit of Market Competition

Entrepreneurship is not just an important function of a market economy. It is a factor of production. The factors of production are used to produce a profit, and the enterprise factor returns are profits from its use. Enterprise and entrepreneurship are two coordinating factors used to assume risks. The eminent Austrian economist, Israel Kirzner, stated, "Entrepreneurship and competition have taught us that the market process is always entrepreneurial. And that the entrepreneurial process is always competitive." [6]

Although not reflective, in one culture or another, competition is an aspect of an economy that has not entirely been viewed by society at large as a congenial activity. Instead of having a cooperative view of competition, most people consider competition to be cutthroat. I think F. A. Hayek would say we have a pretense of competition. That is, we have not figured out the inner workings of competition as a form of cooperation.

---

[6] 6. M. I. Kirzner, *Competition & Entrepreneurship* (City, IL: University of Chicago Press, 1973).

Oddly enough, many of the activities conducted in society are based on some competing forces. The market, as a process and as competition, is an instrument that allows newcomers into a given marketplace. The market operates in continuous motion and does not stop or pause. It is a process of constant buying, selling, producing, and manufacturing of consumer goods, business goods, and services. The process creates circumstances where free entry results in other smaller entrepreneurs competing with incumbent firms.

Why does *competition* evoke a connotation that is antithetical to everyday social life? Alternatively, it is a word we do not hear too often, nor do we often hear about the positive benefits of the market process. If there are no competitors, there are no markets, said Kirzner. If there are no markets, there are no entrepreneurs. If there are no entrepreneurs, we are in trouble. The railroads, America's first big business, was the consequence of fierce competition between entrepreneurs and investors. [7]

If it were not for the competitive rivalry and entrepreneurial ingenuity of enterprises in the late nineteenth century, names like Daniel McCallum and J. Edgar Thomson wouldn't be known. They changed the concepts of line and staff and departmental organizational design. And they perfected the flow of internal communications and monitoring the evaluation of employee performance.

McCallum developed the first organizational chart and the use of the telegraph for organizational units, to

---

[7] 7. A. D. Chandler, *The Visible Hand: The Managerial Revolution in American Business* (Cambridge, MA: Harvard Business Press, 2002).

communicate in real time. These were all new implements to American business. These entrepreneurs played a big part in the discovery of modern management practices, which encouraged the *visible hand* of management in its earliest phase. McCallum and Thomson applied entrepreneurial skills and insights that would later revolutionize management practices, which contemporary firms use to this very day.

This competitive process and entrepreneurial thought and action brought about innovative ideas to later serve the consuming public. Without a competitive process most of our daily products and services would never have fully developed into what we have access to today. Entrepreneurship and innovation gave the visible hand its quantum leap, which later became increasingly bureaucratic and less entrepreneurial. In the same sense, it was competitive forces that allowed ideas to generate—ideas like rate cutting, interfirm competition, use of new technology within the firm, development of local micromarkets, and Pullman sleeping cars.

These segments of history provide the culmination of mass retailing. The innovation and creation by entrepreneurs brought about retailers such as Lord & Taylor, Macy's, John Wanamaker, Bloomingdale's, Nieman Marcus, and Sears. In this same context, competition is, in the words of Kirzner, the ability for newcomers to enter a market freely.

There are numerous views of the term *competition*. This term evokes a picture of instability in a world that should be protected, safe, and predictable. There is a tinge of rivalry and human action or conduct that might be off-putting to some. Would market activity—discovery and awareness— be an essential endeavor if there was no counterpart or place in which it happened? If competition were eliminated from the marketplace due to heavy interventions, how would entrepreneurs learn about missed opportunities?

Henry Ford (of the Ford Motor Company) and William Durant (of General Motors) fiercely competed for decades, attempting to grab the most market share of the automobile industry. But this resulted from low barriers to entry when they entered the auto industry. Ford and Durant both tried to satisfy the wants of those consumers who wanted automobiles. These competing forces led to product differentiation, mass production, consumer financing, corporate managerial structures, and organizational functions.

Competition should be, out of necessity, to serve the social function. Railroads came about because of the stagecoach driver; butchers brought forth slaughterhouses. At times, the term competition is related to the forces of disequilibrium, where plans and knowledge converge and, based on the ability to reach one's plans, determine market efficiency.

How easy is it for market participants to coordinate their plans and reach their goals? This explication of competition extends into many contexts within marketplaces, as the main crux that disallows the freedom of entry. Thus, raising the barriers to entry and the consequences of not reaching one's plans, in a market situation, is the negative effect of competition.

Competition means that not all desires and wishes of individuals will be satisfied, due to the natural market condition called scarcity. But for a society to grow or encourage growth, there is a need for natural resources, labor, knowledge, education, saving, entrepreneurs, and requisite attitudes. We must not forget that any enterprise will not work in an economic market that cannot absorb changes or adjustments—basically, when market forces are fixed. In the same way, if a culture is adverse to change, [8] entrepreneurship cannot flourish.

Cultural groups have, over time, changed or modified their economic patterns to fit new circumstances. This allows new knowledge to affect market opportunities at home or in a new region of the world. But some cultural aspects have, over time, remained the same. As groups of individuals created small- or medium-sized firms, they brought different ideologies there as well.

It is in the market process or the adaptation of different ideologies that competition, in the marketplace, chooses its entrepreneurial leaders. In any economic system, it is the function of competition—not insidious competition but market processes—that allows those who wish to do better to succeed and allows individuals with aspirations to rise through the social ranks as market participants. Competition, in many ways, is the joiner between large and small businesses, in the entrepreneurial sense of the term. This means that most of the innovation and creation of products, before entering the marketplace, are from smaller firms.

There is prominence in the creative role of entrepreneurship. Creativity is the *entrepreneurial hand*, in response to consumer demands. This leads to several questions: Is the cause of economic change the entrepreneurial

---

[8] 8. B. Klein, *Dynamic Economics* (Cambridge, MA: Harvard University Press, 1977).

culture, or is economic change the cause of entrepreneurship? Is it opportunity that entices an entrepreneurial culture, or the conditions, as such, that deter or entice the discovery process?

Individuals can either find creative ways to approach changing situations or adapt to changing circumstances with existing methods. On net balance, it is safe to assume that competition "uncovers, coordinates, and eliminates social maladjustments." [9] This signals to others that new information is in circulation and is aimed at modified market discoveries. The competitive process, in the entrepreneurial sense, creates a congenial culture that brings forth new technology or uses of technology. These new discoveries are surprising and allow newness to diffuse across multiple marketplaces and positively affect human life.

---

[9] 9. H. Soto de Jesus, *The Austrian School Market Order and Entrepreneurial Creativity* (Northampton, MA: Cheltenham: Edward Elgar, 2008).

2

Entrepreneurial Leadership

What is entrepreneurial leadership? Taking both words together provides meaning as to how cultures persist. If entrepreneurship entails the discovery of something new, then its key claim is that leading is the action that opens new opportunities—whether that is for others or for oneself. Entrepreneurial leadership is a far more conducive function in providing people a way to get out of a conventional rut or a cultural pattern—patterns that are no longer useful in purpose and intent.

Maybe Joseph Schumpeter was correct when he said, "If there was no opportunity, there was no occasion for leadership. Class distinctions and social differentiations arise and have meaning only where environmental factors change with sufficient speed, where there is scope for action, decisions, and service." [10]

Are entrepreneurial leaders representative of classes, the shifting of class membership, or at a deeper level, the cultural

---

[10] 10. J. Schumpeter, *The Economics and Sociology of Capitalism* (Princeton, NJ: Princeton University Press, 1991).

underpinning of cultural transmissions over time? Taking this framework, provided by Schumpeter, there seems to be a real way in which cultures and classes are intertwined. Therefore, every class has a specific function that it must fulfill. That is seen through the actions of its members.

Even if there were a standard definition, it would not capture the essence of an individual or group of individuals whose actions, in the marketplace, are directed only to the future, in a lockstep fashion. Aristotle spoke of a prime mover—a force that can be acted upon or a response creating a force. Entrepreneurs do both. They act upon and are adjusters of materials, resources, innovations, and services to humanity. Alexander Shand said,

> Entrepreneurs are those whose acumen enables them to spot opportunities before others. Then, logically, it follows that the largest profits are possible in those societies, in which the economy has previously been in an unsatisfactory state. In the sense that profit opportunities have been going unnoticed. [11]

Throughout entrepreneurial literature, a good deal of evidence shows the positive effects of entrepreneurial leadership in the marketplace. Behaviors in a firm, and their decision-making on investments, creativity, and innovation, are a result of effectively opening and investing so that other

---

[11] 11. A. H. Shand, *The Capitalist Alternative: An Introduction to Neo-Austrian Economics* (New York, NY: New York University Press, 1984).

entrepreneurs can follow in the marketplace. Alexander Shand says that entrepreneurial followers' actions resemble the unitary function of entrepreneurial leaders' visions.

The visions set forth open opportunities and potential discoveries, not in the same way, but in a multitudinous range of entrepreneurial responses that are either *orthodox, unorthodox,* or *heterodox.* The problem is that there is a tendency to assume that the people led by entrepreneurs should or would act the same, respond to visions in the same way, and pursue the same ends based on the influence of entrepreneurial leaders' empowerment, vision, and market strategies. While entrepreneurial leaders may indeed foster market phenomena, market phenomena entail adjustments to production, products, and services and consistent creative development; it cannot be assumed that just because the antecedent of entrepreneurial leadership might be similar that the determinate for each follower is to be the same in response.

Market adjustments, prices, and all the rest are direct results of competing visions, decisions, and actions of entrepreneurs and entrepreneurial followers (i.e., entrepreneurial proxies). Although it is easy to assume that the results of goals, tasks, or actions are the culmination of a single unitary vision emanated from a body of individuals, they might be more the result of a competing set of visions interpreted and acted upon through an entrepreneurial leader's vision that is then transmitted to entrepreneurial followers' imitations in that market path.

This raises new questions concerning how we examine entrepreneurial followers' responses when empowered by entrepreneurial leaders who, by their very nature in a marketplace, create ripples of adjustment in the value and prices of goods and opportunity paths. There is a difference between the two types of entrepreneurial leaders; one is directly driven by market adjustments and discovers what has been unnoticed by others. On the other hand, the followers find and pursue a path created by a prime mover—an entrepreneurial leader.

The premise here is to notice how visions of entrepreneurial leaders and their environments create a constant struggle of what was and what is, and in turn, creating spaces for others to follow in the near future. Many factors determine the congruency between vision and the adaptability or interpretation of vision as seen by entrepreneurial followers in the sense that most ideas and investments are forward-looking. Factors such as time preference, goals, region, culture, knowledge, opportunity costs, technology, and so forth enable entrepreneurial followers to choose to produce a product or a service according to a dichotomy of heterodox (entrepreneurial), orthodox (similar), and unorthodox (innovative) factors. Another way to view the persistence in the transmission of a culture of entrepreneurship is summed up by F. A. Hayek, in the article titled, "The Creative Powers of a Free Civilization":

> Those who take part in the process have little idea why they are doing what they do, and we have no way of predicting who will at each step first make the appropriate move or that particular combinations of knowledge and skill, personal attitudes and circumstances will suggest to some man the

> successful answer or by what channels his
> example will be transmitted to others who
> will follow the lead. [12]

There are innumerable outcomes of entrepreneurial visions, options, and pursuits of entrepreneurial followers who stand on the shoulders of giants. The problem with a quick jump of the gun is that we do not perceive, in many cases, real-life marketplace opportunities and discoveries in very localized ways. The prevailing entrepreneurial narratives do not capture individual perceptions. The whole idea of the market economy and the entrepreneur is to open pathways for others to follow in either the same way (orthodox), in a completely different way (heterodox), or in a similar way but with modifications (unorthodox). An individual's ability to acquire and use capital (tools of productivity) as a means of acquiring entrepreneurial followers must be considered. Without capital (i.e., land, labor, knowledge, etc.), one cannot be as productive as an individual with possession and rights to capital. Capital, however, can be viewed in entirely different ways, but the point is to use implements according to the market path being pursued. Entrepreneurial followers and entrepreneurial leaders must save and use capital in ways that consumers do not. Saving is the key to successfully pursuing marketplace opportunities. John A. Allison said, "If you eat your corn, you will not have any seed corn to plan next year's crop." [13] This statement

---

[12] . A. Kemp, *Essays on Individuality* (Indianapolis, IN: Liberty Fund, 1977).

[13] . J. A. Allison, *The Leadership Crises and the Free Market Cure* (New York, NY: McGraw-Hill, 2015).

emphasizes the importance of saving, investing, and using capital to build a pathway to opportunity—the function of the entrepreneurial leader.

Most people enjoy music and can relate to the music of a particular time. Often, we listen to and enjoy music from another time because of its melody, sound, and energy; or we listen to a new song that is a remix using samples of an older song. Motown Records was a renowned music label and conglomerate of artists from various genres across the music spectrum. The founder (i.e., the entrepreneurial leader) of Motown Records was the world-famous Berry Gordy. Gordy founded Motown in 1959 as a small label of talented artists in genres ranging from rhythm and blues to gospel. Over the decades, these artists, performers, and songwriters made Motown the music icon it is today. A few of these artists are Aretha Franklin, Smokey Robinson, and Diana Ross & The Supremes, whose paths were paved by Gordy. The resources used to catapult several successful musicians and songwriters emanating from the Motown label into entrepreneurial paths was the result of Gordy opening market paths. The same can be said of entrepreneurs like Steve Jobs who created paths for many others to follow and who even created inventions others employed as tools for creating entrepreneurial opportunities. In a different way, entrepreneurial leaders such as Gustavus Swift and Henry Leland paved paths for others such as Henry Ford—whose name is associated with mass production—to follow.

A result of entrepreneurial leadership is that it creates an expansive and innovative economy where the growth of production and productive resources brings forth new ideas through their alternative uses. In this case, and many others alike, the music market elected an entrepreneurial leader as the path creator, for whom all the main ingredients were in place, such as the profit motive, knowledge, attitudes and ideology, savings, and resources. Paths were created, and followers entered these paths that had been opened to them due to prime movers, as Aristotle would have put it. The entrepreneurial follower and the mechanism creating the leader path are predicated on the spontaneous movements of consumer wants. The main idea is that change and adaptability are difficult propositions when people in society are unable to articulate the reason for change or intuitively understand the nature of change. Change—particularly economic change in conventions, institutions, and principles—tends to be unarticulated and painful, slow, and undeliberate. Therefore, it is entrepreneurs who thrive through change and adapt to shifting economic waves and are thus incurring the profits or losses in a world that is riddled with unexpected change.

3

Entrepreneurs Do Not Fail

Failure is a misnomer if we are referring to the human action involved in an entrepreneurial pursuit. A commonly held, although misleading, notion is that entrepreneurs often fail within the first few years in the marketplace. Often, I wonder why and how it happens that entrepreneurs fail only after a few years in the market if they envisioned a profitable opportunity where none had existed beforehand and was *visually* unapparent to others. In a nonmetaphorical sense, let us think about this: entrepreneurs discover and invest in producing and distributing goods for those who demand them the most, thereby creating downward pressures on consumer prices via their purposeful action. With that said, why is it that at one point, the entrepreneur discovers effectual ways to satisfy consumer demands, and only within a few years is the entrepreneur then reported to have failed? I do not buy this one bit, and this belief is all wrong. Here is why: firms measure *success* or *failure* via profit and loss. How do we measure the entrepreneur's contributions? We might measure the entrepreneurial function by its compounding effect on future developments for human flourishing.

Instead of, as some might think, that entrepreneurs quit too soon, the reality is that entrepreneurs are often negatively affected by distortions and interventions in the marketplace. Not to mention, entrepreneurs are subject to the ongoing competition between existing and emerging institutions. Institutional competition is a result of *what has been* and *what will be*. Nevertheless, institutional conditions serve to attract the unknown persons with specific knowledge who are incentivized and motivated to contribute to the knowledge fund of the marketplace.

Some have said that entrepreneurs do not pick the right people for their team, their purposes are directed toward the wrong endeavor, and somehow, they lack commitment, persistence, and all the rest. I do not buy it. We must look at the effects of various institutional changes, distortions, and interventions, which play such a significant role in the assumed failure of nascent or incumbent entrepreneurs. It boggles the mind how failure is attributed in many cases only to entrepreneurs' characteristics instead of being attributed to the distortions and interventions placed in their way that obstruct the signals that are widely used to make decisions. Elements like money and price function as entrepreneurial signals that reflect the knowledge needed to produce and distribute consumer goods and services, particularly those economic goods valued most by market participants who consume and are satisfied by them.

Even the thought of an entrepreneur's failure is somehow self-inflicted is utter nonsense. Who would discover a profitable opportunity only to fail at it knowingly?

Moreover, the same people who attribute failure to the entrepreneur have the antidote for fixing their failures. Ha! We got entrepreneurial failure all wrong. It is no doubt true that sometimes entrepreneurial projects do not cut the mustard. However, according to Murray Rothbard, no one else knows their market and the workings of their market better than the entrepreneur. Therefore, there must be some external factors creating situations conducive to failure. As you see, commentary about entrepreneurial failures seems to face inward—failure is the entrepreneurs' fault—of course. I beg to differ. Firms may fail, but entrepreneurs do not. Entrepreneurs shape our future only by adding to the entrepreneurial stock of knowledge. The steamboat, airplane, vehicles, ice manufacturing, light bulbs, umbrellas, pens, food preparation and processing, digital apps, and technology in general, are all outcomes of an accumulation of knowledge from previous entrepreneurs that took place over decades, and in some cases, even centuries.

Here is a thought experiment: if entrepreneurs functioned under a designated entrepreneurial sector, I presume they would *fail* less often. We know that institutions shape individual's decision-making and, in the entrepreneurial sector, risk tolerance. An entrepreneurial sector as a *fund of knowledge* creates conditions for entry and learning from previous entrepreneurs' accumulated experiences. Institutions of entrepreneurship invite the effectual conditions for human flourishing—the spontaneously grown institutions where wealth can be created *ex nihilo*, out of nothing. You see, the marketplace is not anthropomorphic; it is a means by which individuals can pursue their end. Failure, as implied by those who do not realize it, is one of those misleading words concerning the function of entrepreneurship in a market economy. We cannot look at failure as such. Intervention, distortions, and institutional shifts have more significant effects on entrepreneurial success than the personal characteristics attributed to their failures. Gunderson described the resilient force of wealth creators: "Entrepreneurs detect and pursue opportunities throughout the economy, which is to say, wherever the previous limits of human ingenuity can be extended by further innovations." [14]

---

[14] . G. Gunderson, *The Wealth Creators: An Entrepreneurial History of the United States* (New York, NY: Penguin Books, 1989).

4

Consuming Is Social Coordination of Choice

Writers of articles on consumer spending seem not to want consumers making their own choices about what to buy and how much to buy. Instead, they provide a plan for consumers to avoid what some call excess consumerism. In other words, what some suggest is that *excessive consumption* is terrible for you and everyone else. To put the matter mildly, the concept of excessive consumption has no basis in how people operate in the real world. This view of excessive consumption does not account for the fact that people's goals are not focused on buying stuff. Individuals make individual choices using their income, and they make their own decisions to fulfill their own needs and wants. Real people are not seeking the judgment or moral approval of these writers.

One thing is for sure: people prefer to obtain what they want now rather than later. Real people have time preferences—this statement is far from new. Each of us has time preferences, and we express these preferences in the market, where we make decisions on how we spend our time and income. For example, if I asked you to choose between taking $50 today or $50 in two years, which option would you choose? If you had the option to purchase bread for $1.50 today, would you buy the same loaf of bread tomorrow for $3? These examples clearly show that people make their choices to satisfy their desires under personal time preferences. Unfortunately, the idea of consumerism, or *excessive consumption,* posed by the recent articles clearly shows a widespread misunderstanding of how real people operate in the marketplace.

The Consumer Confidence Board found that consumer confidence has improved since December 2020, including a reported uptick in January 2021, and stated that "consumers' expectations for the economy and jobs advanced further, suggesting that consumers foresee conditions improving in the not-too-distant future." Entrepreneurs' low time preferences are good news for consumers and producers. Consumers are confident in the market conditions for consumption, and guess what—the customer still rules!

Let's face it, the idea of excessive consumption in the aggregate is all wrong. Those who support the notion of excessive consumption do not see human behavior as it is but as how they think it should be. What is essential for a functioning marketplace is not buying more than a writer believes one may need but how people choose to buy more or less of what they want. The market process is about consumers making personal choices using their own time and income to buy what makes them happy and is useful toward their goals. What is wrong with that? I love coffee, and I tend to buy coffee from different places, and I buy beans to make coffee at home. Should a coffee shop owner tell me that I can buy only one bag of coffee because buying three bags of coffee would be excessive? This is true of most things like shoes, streaming movies, and exercise downloads. What may be more for one person can very well be less for someone else.

You see, when it comes to consumption, people tend to decide for themselves what is excessive and what is not. The central proposition for those who do not understand how the market works is that what is excessive to me should be excessive to everyone else in the world. However, excessive consumption cannot go beyond what is produced—as we all know, there is scarcity. Like most people, I want to buy what I deem to be useful, necessary, and valuable. For one thing, consumers are not bumbling idiots—they have goals in mind as they shop for items. Consumers are attentive to prices, needs, timing, and market conditions related to their situation. As long as excessive buying does not harm others or is illegal, they should enjoy an economic system that produces material goods for consumers' purposes and enjoyment. My enjoyment is a hot cup of joe, and your enjoyment may be power tools or clothes. We can enjoy these things because we earn income to buy them, and they bring joy.

Let us get to the point: consumers who *buy excessively* are, in reality, exercising their freedom in the marketplace. Consumers can determine on their own to either buy fewer or more significant amounts of bread; however, if they buy fewer amounts of bread, they will cause the incomes of wheat producers to fall. On the other hand, consumers who purchase more video game downloads raise the incomes of people employed in that industry. Moreover, the opposite effect happens when consumers are told not to make their own choices in the marketplace. Do not buy more than two cups of coffee a day as that is excessive. Ha! We must remember that production takes time. Rome was not built overnight, and neither were the items bought in-person or online by millions of people every day. That means if less is purchased, less will be produced in the future.

Producers and manufacturers determine what to make more or less of based on market demand. Demand begets production. The market provides for those who are willing to buy, and people who are unwilling to buy do not stimulate production. Producers accommodate mass demand with scarce resources. Consumption is a balance of scarcity and abundance, and the outcome creates more choices for consumers. You see, economic thriving does not revolve around buying stuff; it is the outcome of consumer choice.

Overall, excessive consumption may not fulfill some people's desires, but it may bring true happiness for some people. People who buy—whether excessively or not—fulfill their economic roles of supporting business owners and their local communities. To assert that consumers should stop excessively buying products assumes away the prospect that people do not change shopping patterns or increase family sizes over time. I was always told that you do not bite the hand that feeds you. The market is the only social place where the coordination between consumers and producers can facilitate goals and mutually beneficial choices for everyone involved via the buying process. These excessive purchases fuel the economy, which helps all people flourish and live their best lives.

5

Cast Down Your Bucket Where You Are

How can institutions such as education, family, language, laws, and economy be understood as catalysts for emerging institutions of entrepreneurship?

From an entrepreneurial perspective, institutions result from emerging social phenomena based on subjective experiences and perspectives. Institutions of entrepreneurship include action, technology, knowledge and learning, culture, and values. You see, institutions of entrepreneurship do not thwart marketplace initiatives; instead, they are instrumental for entrepreneurial action to advance into the near future. Many of our institutions are the result of human action and not of design, but over time, predetermined narratives tend to come into existence. From an entrepreneurial point of view, set narratives of entrepreneurship are guided toward a general framework of individual potentialities and should not be deterministic. Institutions serve as constraints and, at the same time, as action enablers.

As in all entrepreneurial matters, subjectivity applies.

The subjectivity of entrepreneurial institutions should allow individuals the ability to take advantage of newly emerging market opportunities. If nascent entrepreneurs go about serving others in the marketplace in the same ways that previous actors had done, they will get the same results. As a case in point, it was Einstein who changed Isaac Newton's longtime theory of gravity by pointing out that there is a special and a general relativity. Einstein replaced Newton's theory, not by using the same thoughts and processes as Newton, but from his subjective institutional experiences, knowledge, and skills that he possessed at a particular point in time as new ideas emerged. The theory of relativity gave physics a massive leap in science. The conventions of physics allowed Einstein to use the institutional framework to discover and attempt to be part of something useful for scientists and the layperson. Can we extend this same sentiment to the entrepreneur to advance using the institutions of entrepreneurship? I say yes! An entrepreneur's experience within institutional environments is subjective, so in the words of Booker T. Washington, nascent entrepreneurs should "cast down your bucket where you are." Ideally, everyone should have the opportunity to cast down a bucket where they are, particularly via emerging entrepreneurial institutions, as a means to learn from the marketplace and participate in the market economy.

Emerging entrepreneurial institutions—such as starting a business on the Internet—are the key to entry into markets that may have once been unobtainable for some people, primarily because institutions are subjectively experienced. In many ways, institutions can be identity-producing. If Mary Kay started her business a certain way, it does not mean others following her footsteps have to do it the same way to be as successful as she was. Like Isaac Newton, she inspired others. Emerging entrepreneurial institutional environments, for those individuals steeped in institutional identity, provide a chance for individuals to realize alternatives to the normative ways of participating in each marketplace.

Moreover, nascent entrepreneurs can use emerging institutions via institutional superhighways through multiple technological devices (i.e., smartphones, laptops, social media, and e-commerce platforms) to make transaction-based sales that can serve consumers across the globe. Institutional environments ought to allow everyone the chance to pursue their entrepreneurial plans. As we know, plans are often diverted due to unexpected events, which is why entrepreneurial institutional environments should serve as market feedback mechanisms and not barriers to market entry. Dropping a bucket means using production factors to serve consumers in the best possible way, not waiting for the ideal circumstance to participate in the marketplace. Entrepreneurs should not wait for an ideal situation, ideal investment, or the perfect business idea.

Within the institutions of entrepreneurship, one should be able to *drop down their bucket where they are*. Institutions of entrepreneurship should make room for new entrepreneurial participants via technological devices (i.e., smartphones, tablets, and laptops). Higher levels of entrepreneurship are not the cause but the effect of technological advancements. Technology is not static but dynamic, and the same can be said for the people using it. Capital resources of all kinds are primarily not only to save labor but to increase the firm's output.

A recent report showed that 14 percent of business owners are between the ages of thirty and thirty-nine, and 4 percent are between eighteen and twenty-nine years old. These demographics (especially those aged eighteen to twenty-nine) own smartphones or laptops with access to e-commerce platforms and digital media—access to consumer markets at their fingertips. The next logical question is: if 13 percent of millennials spend over twelve hours on their phones daily, how can they participate in the marketplace? The data speak to the fact that everyone has the chance to drop their buckets where they are and serve their fellow man.

"At least 81% of entrepreneurs do not have access to a bank loan or venture capital," said a recent Kauffman Foundation report. The report indicated, "Very little of the total capital flow to entrepreneurs is geared toward women and people of color." Again, institutional environments are entirely subjective, as there is too much diversity among people and circumstances to assume that everyone interested in entrepreneurship might uniformly enter the market and participate evenly. Nevertheless, that is the point! Instead of institutional barriers preventing entrepreneurship, institutions of entrepreneurship and emerging institutions ought to function as superhighways of entrepreneurial accessibility via the means of one's talent and resources where they are, as indeed most people have access to technological devices.

There are 272.6 million smartphone users across the United States alone, which means that 272.6 million business opportunities are waiting for people to drop down their buckets. Not to mention, 52.4 percent of the population worldwide uses their smartphones to access the Internet.

Entrepreneurship is a function of the market process, an activity that should be open to anyone willing to serve others' needs. Internet searches are now an institution; they are how people express needs. There are vast amounts of these Internet searches, providing the inquisitive entrepreneurial mind with a million ways to start a business. However, the problem is that not all potential entrepreneurs will experience the same institutional environments uniformly. We all have different plans and expectations of how entrepreneurial institutions should facilitate entrepreneurial pursuits, whether they are in music, art, lectures, reading materials, cooking lessons, painting services, or exercise tutorials. If buckets are dropped where the person is, the only cost incurred by the nascent entrepreneur is time, and chances are that someone got served, which is the first step toward the ideal success narrative that we often associate with entrepreneurship.

There are entrepreneurial opportunities only if entrepreneurial institutional environments create entry for anyone willing to drop their bucket where they are. Entrepreneurial institutions should operate as uncertainty reducers and not uncertainty enhancers. Therefore, the conventional institutional environments ought to support emerging entrepreneurial opportunities and individual action. The institutions of entrepreneurship should accommodate action in emerging institutions so that the enterprising spirit can pour the horn of plenty on all of us.

6

The Rise of the Consumer-Entrepreneur

Marginal and well-meaning small businesses leave the marketplace when there are swings in the economy. Many consumers want to patronize these businesses, but the current economic situation calls for consumers to adjust and make trade-offs in their consumption patterns. The inability of small businesses to offer services and products may well lead consumers to take on a new role in the marketplace—as consumer-entrepreneur. DIY entrepreneurs are individuals who use their resources, apply them, and bring them to marketplaces via e-platforms by way of business-to-consumer (B2C), consumer-to-consumer (C2C), and business-to-business (B2B) sectors.

The economic situation poses new realities regarding how changing economic conditions and ensuing marketplace transformations affect consumer thinking regarding service and product acquisitions in the long run. The marketplace may shift as an unintended consequence of consumers' changed attitudes. There are digital options, but there is also an array of services that are not in a digitized format, especially some service-oriented acquisitions such as hairstyles and cuts, dental work, cosmetics, vehicle maintenance, and the like. The products and services that consumers have historically received from small businesses in the past will, in many cases, no longer be available as the economic picture and players shift toward its more productive areas of industry. These market changes must alter consumer actions regarding product and service acquisitions in a far-reaching way that we have yet to see.

The immediate effects of the economy are small business closures and the pivot to the online acquisition of economic goods and digital services. However, we often do not consider the long-term effects that are not yet visible based on the changes in customers' behaviors as they decide how to adjust to the fact that fewer options are available. To this point, Thomas Sowell once said that people are not blocks of wood; they react to changes in ways never intended. Economic shifts in the short run have in the past forced some cultural groups to become entrepreneurs. In some limited cases, entrepreneurship was, for many, the only choice available to them.

The DIY entrepreneur-consumer uses their human capital, skills, resources, and networks within social and digital platforms to market their creations. DIY entrepreneurs have digital platforms to reach many more consumers than the average entrepreneur had fifty years ago as they can now set up a virtual store via Amazon, Etsy, Instagram, and other platforms. To put it simply, the consumer-entrepreneur is an individual who produces the product or service themselves and sells their product to other consumers in a consumer-to-consumer marketplace. Not all DIY options are the best or worst, but the rise of digitalpreneurship is a manifestation given the changing consumers' choices under marketplace phenomena; that is, people respond to changes and the changes are reflected in the marketplace.

Many consumers have experienced a market transition in which they do projects themselves; that is, they have accessed their ability to produce products and services they would have otherwise had to search for and find in the marketplace. Digital entrepreneurship has its advantages; while many owners of capital experienced the adverse effects of an economy that forces innovation on the existing marketplace, consumers have found ways of doing things themselves and providing their services to others in an emerging consumer-to-consumer marketplace—C2C, B2C, or B2B. The visible effect of any market resistant to entrepreneurship is fewer and fewer small business providers in the marketplace, but the invisible secondary effect is that this dissipation creates a consumer-entrepreneurial culture. C2C via e-platforms, or B2B, are relationships in a given marketplace ecosystem where individual consumers sell to and buy from other business consumers with other business entities.

There is no doubt that the horn of plenty for at-home consumption via digital products and platforms has fulfilled consumers' desires, but there are some services where consumers must take part in their acquisition. Surely consumers can order most products online and download digital products and some digital services, but what about the services where the acquiring consumer must play an active part in its consumption? People would love to have dental work performed virtually because it would save the pain of an actual visit, but this is not a service that one can accomplish (DIY) at home. As another example, I cannot get my hair styled or cut virtually, but I can do it myself in the comfort of my own home. I cannot get my car oil changed if my mechanic closes his doors. I guess I can do it myself.

If we look past the immediate benefits of our digitized consumption and think about the secondary effects, there is a significant additional array of consumers' choices, particularly their choice to DIY and engage in entrepreneurship. Whether or not consumer-entrepreneurship is good, we do not know. Optimistically speaking, individuals who never thought of DIY and becoming a consumer-entrepreneur can now reap the benefits of the digital marketplace.

The simple fact is that if my mechanic closes his shop, I will have to maintain my vehicle myself. If my barber closes his business, I will have to style and cut my hair myself, which will not look the best, but the alternative is even less appealing. The short-run visible effects are the number of technological platforms that will allow consumers to DIY and e-commerce platforms to engage in consumer-to-consumer exchanges for their wants, leading to an increasing number of consumer-entrepreneurs. The long-run effect is that consumers will have a new role in the future market economy, which we have not intended—the DIY consumer-entrepreneur.

In the long run, small businesses decrease their market presence, allowing more consumers to become more productive in satisfying their wants and those of others, which creates robust C2C, B2C, or B2B marketplaces. The immediate effect will be to show that consumers are creative and can be entrepreneurial. In the long run, will consumers make these timely trade-offs between their leisure and production and overcome the disutility of their labor to DIY their services and produce goods for themselves and others in the B2C, B2B, or C2C marketplaces? Only time will tell if economic swings and adjustments have short- or long-run economic impact and whether either market force will have lasting effects on consumers' ability and willingness to increase DIY entrepreneurship.

7

The Good Entrepreneur

I suggest that to be good, a business should not pursue profit and, along with it, customer satisfaction. Ignoring the profit motive is deemed more important than the entrepreneurial reward of profit that comes from providing a service or product to customers who demand value. The bad entrepreneur is only concerned with making money, surviving in the market, and serving consumers. The bad entrepreneur pursues charitable deeds but not at the cost of what consumers demand. You see, being the good entrepreneur only helps a few concentrated groups but ignores the diffuse effects of many consumers, profit rewards, and potential failure. What is the good entrepreneur to do?

Let us be honest. If the entrepreneur is not primarily motivated by profit, what happens if the business fails or can no longer service its customers due to profits invested in nonmarket activities that do not serve them? Unfortunately, there is a public perception that does not allow entrepreneurs to pursue only a profit motive, because others must choose for them—they call them good entrepreneurs. They call them good if they subordinate the profit motive to lofty, nonmarket, charitable endeavors outside the scope of producing consumer value.

Profit guides resources to their highest valued uses as determined by people's wants and desires. Should entrepreneurs disregard the profit motive, making it secondary, and replace it with nonmarket motives? What would the effect of nonmarket motives be on the entrepreneur and the customer? When Coca-Cola changed its formula, it was because of customer preference. Consumer preference was a warning sign to the *potential* loss of profit, which caused the company to bring back the original formula! Good entrepreneurs focus on nonmarket motives— endeavors that are outside their division of labor in the first place. Ludwig von Mises once asked, what is the good entrepreneur to do?

Should not the primary goal of the entrepreneur be to remain profitable so that, at a minimum, they can run their business and continue production, which then serves customers who choose to buy their products and services? Don't entrepreneurs deserve to earn a reward for taking risks and putting their livelihoods in jeopardy to procure materials and goods to bring to the market? To eliminate the profit motive is to ask entrepreneurs to provide their vital services to consumers at a higher cost than they would otherwise. Profit is the reward given by satisfied customers and a market signal of what to do more of and what to do less of. You see, the good entrepreneur, not having a profit motive, primarily focuses on motives that do not serve customer needs. For example, your local pizzeria owner does not know you personally, but they know that you want hot, delicious pizza. That is their motive. Fortunately for the pizzeria owner, there is a reward for preparing that pizza for you. However, if your local pizzeria owner does not profit, they will no longer exist in your community to serve pizza. End of story.

Therefore, we must ask: are good entrepreneurs, motivated not by profit but by nonmarket issues, likely to be successful and stay in business? Why is there an expectation that entrepreneurs run a business without a profit motive? They cannot. The *good* entrepreneurs are nonmarket-oriented and put profits into nonmarket endeavors aside from producing value for their customer; these nonmarket motives are placed before the profitability of the business and a value-added process for customers.

Having a motive other than profit poses a critical problem. Mises asked, "How can a conscientious entrepreneur persuade a banker or a capitalist to lend him money if he himself cannot see any prospect of a profitable return on his investment?" The good entrepreneur, in fact, must ignore customers and forgo profit for nonmarket activity, in which the entrepreneur has a great chance of failing due to financial instability and loss of customers.

When the profit motive is taken off the table as a primary objective, there are several consequences. There ceases to be a way to reward the entrepreneur over and above the costs of doing business. Someone must bear the consequence if the business is not profitable and struggles financially. Customers leave.

Good or bad entrepreneurs, if they wish, can be motivated by things other than profit. The question remains: what cost are they willing to pay to keep the business from failing? Indeed, other motives can come into play, but does the entrepreneur who decides not to do what is in vogue become a *bad* entrepreneur? Survival of the business comes first; serving consumers comes next. If good entrepreneurs fail, who subsidizes them? If bad entrepreneurs survive and continue to provide value, are they not doing what they are rewarded to do? Bad entrepreneurs can choose what they want to do with their profits if it does not interfere with market exchanges and customer satisfaction.

There is nothing better than to support one's community and do good deeds for others. However, we must examine a simple fact: if an entrepreneur is not driven by profit first, then a profit-driven entrepreneur will come along, do things better at a better price, and obtain a greater market share. This is a fact of the market process. The problem comes when the good entrepreneur is asked to be guided by nonmarket activities, as Mises stated. He said that entrepreneurs are viewed as *hard* and *selfish* if they are guided by a market position instead of a nonmarket position, and he asked: what is the good entrepreneur supposed to do?

How soon we forget that, as Mises noted, it is the "consumers and not the entrepreneurs that determine the direction and scope of production." To serve customers, entrepreneurs must maintain a profitable operation—this is what a *good* entrepreneur does. If the entrepreneur chooses to disregard the profit motive, customers will not be served. If they are served, at what cost? Some expect to interfere with an entrepreneur's business endeavor to pressure them to provide nonmarket outcomes. They expect the entrepreneur to run a business without a profit. But the same people demand products and services from the entrepreneur. The nonmarket profit motive does not work.

The entrepreneur operates in a market economy, where consumer signals regulate businesses' production or service offerings. Is it feasible to ask that entrepreneurs use their privately held resources for nonmarket endeavors regardless of the profit motive? Should I ask my favorite pizzeria owner to not be motivated by profit, yet demand he keep making those hot, yummy pizzas? Whatever motive the entrepreneur decides to assume, there surely will be a *market consequence.* Nonmarket pressure groups demand that *good* entrepreneurs only be motivated by what *they* think is important, or by the latest nonmarket trend. The fact is, as individuals, entrepreneurs can decide what motivates them and then pursue the means to that end. The main concern should not be whether the entrepreneur is primarily motivated by profit, but the diffuse effects on customers. Further examination is needed as to the costs in the market.

How do motives that are not based on profits bring results in a market economy? Does a secondary motivation other than profit negatively affect the survival of the good entrepreneur or consumers? If so, then it is safe to assume that the demands of consumers can be ignored when there are no bottom-line constraints of profits.

Part 2

Principles, have a way of asserting themselves even
if they are not explicitly recognized but are only
implied in particular decisions, or if they are present
only as vague ideas of what is or is not being done.

—F. A. Hayek (1945)

There is a strong assumption that the only way is the way
that has been. New ways of doing things are often stumbled
upon as they seep into an existing system or how society sees
fit—most often initiated and envisioned by the individual.
Individualism and entrepreneurship are strongly related to
one another. The meaning of individualism has changed
over time, and confusion surrounding the true meaning
and idea is entirely different than it was before. What is
meant in this book about individualism is the use and
application of one's knowledge as seen fit for the best use
within one's social life. Individuals beg the question: what
is the purpose of one's actions? Individualism speaks to
the combination of people creating, collaborating ideas,
exchanging goods, and innovating things via a market
process which supersedes any one person's knowledge if the

same people had conducted things separately. In the strictest sense of individualism, the individual ought to choose to follow a path of entrepreneurship.

As a counterintuitive measure, I ask what the world would be like without entrepreneurs. There must be a history, attitude, and ideology that is in lockstep with the tenets of a given society that nourishes the role of the individual in the formation of assuming the risk of entrepreneurship—tenets that society needs to flourish, at least if the function of an enterprising culture is to subsist for everyday people.

There are, however, particular principles of an entrepreneurial economy that correspond to cultural aspects of society—what is believed and heard, interpreted from the needs of others, marketplace prices, and selling and buying, and then reinterpreted by expectations of the entrepreneur. General principles in an entrepreneurial economy hold through time until society stumbles upon a newer principle that guides society and works better for the effectiveness and continuation of the culture of entrepreneurship. There is a strong pretense to believe that the *visible hand* will take the place of the *entrepreneurial hand*. Discoveries of the entrepreneurial hand happen in *invisible* and *spontaneous* ways in which no one person intends.

Case in point, James Bradley (1693–1762), an English astronomer and priest, was known for two major discoveries in astronomy: the aberration of light and the nutation of the Earth's axis. His discovery of the most effective measurement of the *stellar parallax* was made not with the intention of this fact but while attempting to discover an unexplained cyclical motion known as the aberration of light. Oddly enough, his discoveries occurred while he was sailing on a boat. What is revealing about this case is the happenstance and individual awareness that led to the discovery:

> Calculation showed that if there has been any appreciable motion due to parallax, then the star should have reached its most southerly apparent position in December, and its most northerly apparent position in June. What Bradley found instead was an apparent motion that reached its most southerly point in March, and its most northerly point in September; and that could not be accounted for by parallax; and that cause of a motion with the pattern actually seen was at first obscure. [15]

What one believes and perceives transfers into a particular action. Individuals are part of a process within institutions that set the framework for expecting uncertain changes in an entrepreneurial economy. Alertness and awareness on their own can be affected by the very institutional framework in which the discovery takes place. That is, if the three are barriers to knowledge or marketplaces, then it would be a challenge for an enterprising individual to transmit their knowledge and to use the motivation to pursue an entrepreneurial hunch. Entrepreneurship is not a deliberate action within a process. It always hinges on the potentiality of something new to implement for future gain stemming from the fundamental function not withstanding alternative institutional frameworks.

---

[15] . S. R. Ball, *Great Astronomers: James Bradley* (Columbia, SC: Independent Publishers, 2021).

8

A World without Entrepreneurs

What would the world be like without entrepreneurs? Given that entrepreneurs are central to the market system, a world without entrepreneurs—or with only a few of them—would be a less than desirable situation for humanity. Without entrepreneurs, we would see few new products, little innovation, and few gains in the standard of living. And without entrepreneurs, we would still be using archaic technologies and services. The consumer would have no expectation of regularly finding new and improved products available to him. Innovation might exist in a scientific sense, but the benefits would not be reaped in the marketplace because no entrepreneurs would seek to find ways to make scientific innovations profitable.

Consider how our world has been built by entrepreneurs. Most of what we purchase and use daily started in the minds of entrepreneurs, with their energy and capital. They thought of consumers' needs and wants and brought products into existence with continually more reasonable and affordable prices, making these products available to all people. Let us look at a few specific examples.

Toothpaste, floss, and toothbrushes were invented by William Colgate; the elevator was brought to us by Elisha Otis; and the printing press was accelerated by Richard March Hoe, who invented the rotary printing press. The printed book, laptop or smartphone you use to read this book was made available by a host of entrepreneurs acting to provide you with this capability. Your morning brew from the local coffee shop was served by a conveniently located shop and poured into an easy-to-use cup by entrepreneurs who used their capital and produced and delivered coffee beans to you—from bean to cup. All of this was done in the pursuit of profit.

The list goes on as to the benefits entrepreneurs have brought us and the progress they have made in the lives of the average person who enjoys these conveniences spun out by the market process, competition, and ingenuity. Without entrepreneurs, only the most minimal needs would be fulfilled in the marketplace. The consumer would rarely have a voice—that is, they would have no vote in what products are brought to market. If it were not for entrepreneurs' insistence in meeting consumer demands and expectations, we would still be using rotary phones!

Additionally, it is unlikely that companies would exist in such vast numbers to serve customers. Firms exist to allow entrepreneurs to harness the potential of innovations and turn it into profit. Moreover, entrepreneurial firms help accelerate innovation. In *Inventing the Electronic Century*, Alfred Chandler explained how technology-focused industries started as entrepreneurial spin-offs directed toward expanding innovation even further:

> Those earlier industries were based on a number of basic technological innovations: the electricity-producing dynamo, which brought the electric lighting that transformed urban life, and electric power, which so transformed industrial production techniques; the telephone, which brought the first voice transmission over distances; the internal combustion engine, which produced the automobile and the airplane; the new chemical technologies that permitted the production of man-made dyes and, of more significance, a wide range of man-made therapeutic drugs, and other man-made materials ranging from silicon and aluminum to a wide variety of plastics. [16]

As Chandler explained, the consumer electronics market would not have started *ex nihilo*—out of nothing—without entrepreneurial-minded people within the firms or without consumers demanding new and innovative products.

---

[16] . Alfred Chandler provided a number of examples of how companies pursued innovation and used entrepreneurial decision-making to gain market share. Chandler explained that the learning path is what firms use to innovate for future gains; if they stop learning or discontinue learning paths, they are no longer competitive. See https://hbswk.hbs.edu/item/alfred-chandler-on-the-electronic-century.

Market feedback from consumers enables firms to produce the products consumers demand, and entrepreneurs attempt to use these firms to learn from the marketplace. This is a central process to expanding the market for goods and services since, as Hayek so famously stated, "The market process is discovery through trial and error."

Yet, it is amazing how this critical function of the market is taken for granted: without it, there would be few inventions or innovations—and even less market competition. And, of course, entrepreneurs provide benefits to groups other than consumers. Consider the role of an employer—the one who provides employment to those wanting to earn a livelihood. Commerce and e-commerce would break down along with the division of labor, resulting in a decline in related industries and markets. When the marketplace functions freely, more entrepreneurship today leads to more tomorrow—and benefits the consumer.

For example, if the Great Atlantic and Pacific Tea Company (A&P) had not started the supermarket revolution of its day, many of the products and services consumers now expect as a part of the grocery shopping experience might not exist: no home delivery, self-checkout, coupons, a wide variety of foodstuffs, and one-stop shopping. Expansion in these areas has led to new opportunities for both workers and other entrepreneurs.

We can see similar benefits across an enormous number of new industries. The products, services, and innovations that exist have not magically appeared. They have been the results of decades—if not centuries—of entrepreneurial actions that have built on each other and expanded choices in consumption, employment, and investment—year in and year out.

9

A Culture and History of Entrepreneurship

Most of the market activities in which entrepreneurs are engaged are readily seen. People buy and sell things or provide services at locations to paying customers. But if we examine the unseen activities, we will learn how entrepreneurship is a perpetuating market process. More entrepreneurs tend to create more entrepreneurship, both among themselves and by setting the stage for the creation of *new* entrepreneurs. That is, a population with few entrepreneurs produces few entrepreneurs. A population with *more* entrepreneurs produces even more entrepreneurs.

The real-world view of the world requires a clear understanding that ideology and attitude play a major part in understanding the role of the entrepreneur, and more importantly, their function. Becoming an entrepreneur requires the knowledge and insight that comes from being aware of previous market errors—the errors made in the trial and error of entrepreneurs who came before. Errors and missed opportunities generate market knowledge and information for future entrepreneurs. This is good news! If past entrepreneurs had not served their customers, made mistakes, combined inventions, transformed innovations into usable products, and finally became successes, then others would not consider pursuing entrepreneurship. There would be no such path to self-ownership.

It takes entrepreneurs to produce entrepreneurs. We cannot imagine a world without them. Therefore, it is not just the immediate consequences of hampering markets which makes self-ownership difficult for entrepreneurs. We must also examine the secondary effects on potential entrepreneurs of eliminating paths to entrepreneurship in the long run. Up-and-coming entrepreneurs must do three things: (1) choose an entrepreneurial path that already exists, (2) be mindful that there are market errors waiting to be made, and (3) find insights made by previous entrepreneurs.

Where there is an economic climate for entrepreneurship, where one can hit the ground running, entrepreneurship naturally flourishes and prospers. A rise in propensity for entrepreneurship and self-ownership results in more business model imitation and makes the market ripe for one to follow in others' footsteps. The saying "the greatest form of flattery is imitation" rings true for aspiring entrepreneurs who may hesitate in pursuing profitable market opportunities due to a lack of insight.

In many cases, entrepreneurship has been suppressed or smothered by interventionist and anti-market policies which make it extremely difficult for many would-be entrepreneurs to identify a starting point to enter the market. This creates disincentives for new entrepreneurs to enter the market and pick up where others have left off. Thus, innovation and self-ownership are more likely to prosper in an environment where there is a *history* of entrepreneurship.

The market economy will always possess one relationship: the one between entrepreneurs and consumers. One will serve the other—the entrepreneur will serve the customer. The consumer will look for the entrepreneur who does it better. Just because it has been done before does not mean you cannot do it over again or imitate it. Do not just think outside the box, make the box bigger! The pizza restaurant has been replicated for centuries, but because of previous entrepreneurs' mistakes, others have started pizza restaurants with their own spin. The restaurant owners down the street from you saw someone else do it and decided to do it differently.

Randall Holcombe said, "The connection between entrepreneurship and economic growth is that these previously unnoticed profit opportunities must come from somewhere." [17] There will always be entrepreneurs who make errors in the market that produce insights for others to discover. The beauty of a free-market system is that it creates opportunity for others. When a business misses an opportunity, another one can close the gap by making the product or service better. The critical question is: will there ever be a time when the market produces no errors? No.

Holcombe explained the critical role of entrepreneurial insights—insights that manifest themselves in the actions and thoughts of future entrepreneurs. F. A. Hayek advised that entrepreneurs must be able to act on these insights to

[17] . G. R Holcombe, *Advanced Introduction to the Austrian School of Economics* (North Hampton, MA: Edward Elgar Publishing, 2014).

continue in entrepreneurship. Entrepreneurs pick up market insights and pursue improvement through awareness, discovery, and knowledge. Future entrepreneurs must understand that, even though it has been done before, it can be done again. I hear it all the time from people who say, "I had a good business idea. But it's already been done." Do not let this stop you. Market insights provide other entrepreneurs the opportunity to close the market gap by creating a product or performing a service better than the entrepreneur who came before them. Insights are learned and market gaps are closed because of a favorable economic climate and a long history of entrepreneurial insights scattered like bits of data in the form of feedback across populations.

If you are thinking about becoming an entrepreneur, know that your entrepreneurial predecessors have left behind insights that are waiting for you to notice and grasp. Glean from the errors, mistakes, and missed market opportunities of others to create a better product or service for the consumer.

10

Let Market Conditions Decide: The Ideal Age of an Entrepreneur

The condition of the market economy is the most critical aspect of an entrepreneur's success, not the entrepreneur's age. Yet, there are those who say the opposite; that there is a golden age of entrepreneurial success, and it is forty-five. The combination of the age of the entrepreneur and the right mindset is said to be the perfect formula for market success.

While I agree that everything takes time, I am not convinced that age and mindset are essential for successful entrepreneurial endeavors in the long run. Although age and mindset have a role in success, we cannot disregard the requisite market conditions that are more likely to produce favorable or unfavorable results regardless of age and mindset. Entrepreneurs need a favorable market that rewards their risk-taking. If would-be entrepreneurs who are not in their golden age today are advised to wait to see success when they enter their forties, even under unfavorable market conditions, we are in danger of eliminating one of the economy's critical functions—entrepreneurship itself.

Conventional thinking about entrepreneurship is changing before our very eyes. For example, there have been significant declines in small business ownership and new start-ups, and fewer unicorns decade over decade. Why? Let us say that Rome was not built overnight, and neither was the entrepreneur. Products take time to produce; it takes time to develop a network of customers; it takes time for the entrepreneur to develop awareness; it takes time to find the market error that can be turned into an opportunity; and finally, it takes time for the market to adjust to changes in consumers' tastes, preferences, and perceptions. Entrepreneurs do not acquire human capital in just one day, nor were economic systems created in one day.

Entrepreneurship is a social phenomenon that manifests itself through the passing of time, the application of human energy and capital, and favorable market conditions. No group of people sat around one day and created our market economy; it took vast amounts of experiences and knowledge to come together, creating a space for the entrepreneurial function to operate for us. If the prime age is forty-five, and there have been declines in new entrepreneurial births, who will the newcomers follow? How will the ranks fill with those who can imitate the paths of successful entrepreneurs or small business owners?

The favorable conditions of a market economy are essential so that an individual at any age can find and pursue meaning in life. The benefit of favorable market conditions is to allow would-be entrepreneurs to find meaningful ways of applying their human capital to serve society's most urgent needs, making conditions better for other market participants. The market provides a means by which one entrepreneur pursuing their own aims can enable someone else with whom they have no direct contact to pursue their own goals. In other words, productivity begets productivity. Another benefit of a favorable market economy is that it brings forth visible adjustments, errors, new knowledge, and information against which entrepreneurs can weigh their subjective opportunity costs in assessing the risk of pursuing an opportunity.

Individuals accumulate entrepreneurial skills and opportunity awareness, but they have to act to put them to practical use, and if they cannot, society pays the costs. The costs amount to a decrease in new entrepreneurship, innovations, and knowledge. People pursue endeavors when they are incentivized to do so, and if they are not, it will leave a gap in one of the most critical market functions—entrepreneurship. Rome was built through the experiences and knowledge set in motion by many people over time. F. A. Hayek stated:

> The successful combination of knowledge and aptitude is not selected by common deliberation, by people seeking a solution to their problems through joint effort; it is the product of individuals imitating those who have been more successful and from their being guided by signs or symbols, such as prices offered for their products or expressions of moral or aesthetic esteem for their having observed standards of conduct—in short, of their using the results of the experiences of others. [18]

---

[18] . F. A. Hayek, *The Constitution of Liberty* (Chicago, IL: University of Chicago Press, 1978).

An open economic system, where individuals of all ages (younger, older, and in between) are encouraged to pursue their economic interests considering their subjective opportunity costs, ipso facto is likely to increase new entrepreneurial births. Therefore, the condition of the market economy is a necessary factor for entrepreneurs to maximize their range of choices and ideas, and to discover and innovate. A favorable economic system provides individuals in a society a way to use their human capital to achieve society's needs, on behalf of people they will never know directly. Certainly, age and experience play to the entrepreneur's advantage, but what matters most is the market economy's conditions.

How will people who are not at the golden age react to the current market conditions? They need a measurable market indicator—others' successes. Who will fill the shoes of the entrepreneurs and small business owners who have vanished? We must remember that Rome was not built overnight, and neither was the entrepreneur and the system in which they operate.

11

Entrepreneurship for the Younger Generations

When you were young, did you gain knowledge and learn skills that gave you the human capital necessary to become an entrepreneur or a small business owner? Human capital consists of the knowledge and habits developed as a youngster that form skill sets that can be used later in life in the business world. These skills are developed either through the family unit, culture, or regional location and determine the success or failure of entrepreneurial pursuits and performance. In the young, the development of skills and knowledge are applicable to future ventures in entrepreneurship or small business ownership.

Everything learned from family conversations at the dinner table or through one's culture serve to build some human capital. Across the globe, the people of various regions cultivate certain skills that enable individuals to consider entrepreneurship as a viable choice of work. Some of you never had the social or family settings that gave you entrepreneurial insights. Some people get this while they are young, and some do not. Acquiring human capital at a certain age bolsters the chance of entering entrepreneurship or small business ownership. If human capital or business insights are not embedded culturally or acquired at a certain point, some individuals will never consider entrepreneurship or be successful at it.

We cannot all become successful entrepreneurs, especially if only a few of us come from a cultural background that rewards an ethic of hard work and related values versus a cultural background in which achieving entrepreneurial success is never even thought of. What is valued in the family unit and what is rewarded or praised contributes to an individual's future entrepreneurial skills attainment. Ludwig von Mises noted, "The inequality of men, which is due to differences both in their inborn qualities and in the vicissitudes of their lives, manifests itself." The region of the world in which one lives and the context of the acquired human capital skills are equally vital to the return on an entrepreneurial skill set.

We hear from many entrepreneurs, and those who are not entrepreneurs per se, that much of their education occurred around the family dinner table, or that they lived in a place where small business activity was plentiful. In no way is this the only place or format in which education can be had, but it is a relevant one. Human capital that is based on family, culture, and regional differences has consequential effects for many considering entrepreneurship.

Cultural factors are critical in developing entrepreneurship. Often these cultural factors are overshadowed by the technical aspects of operating a business—the seen versus the unseen. Parents and the elderly pass on their values to their children, values such as taking risks, being independent, challenging uncertainty, etc. Children who are rewarded or not rewarded will either be encouraged or discouraged to pursue entrepreneurial activities in the marketplace. If a child is never taught to be independent, how is he or she able to systemically identify potential profit opportunities and bring those opportunities to fruition?

Habits form over time, and many are culturally based. In some cultures, some children spend up to twelve hours a day playing video games and entertaining themselves on social media. In other cultures, children are expected to work long hours helping their parents with their business or studying to earn the best grade on a school exam. These youths may work at an uncle's garage learning about the mechanics of vehicles or attend college to gain the same business knowledge but in a structured format. In either situation, these youths are learning about private property, e-commerce, revenues, profit and loss, bookkeeping, and so on; they are gaining skill sets and knowledge to run a business of their own in the future.

Whatever is cultivated in the family unit or transmitted culturally will manifest and have consequences in the marketplace (both beneficial and not so beneficial). The youth who acquires a work ethic and values related to entrepreneurial success will have an advantage over their peers who have not had the same experiences. Those who have never learned or acquired the skills and the know-how needed to pursue entrepreneurship or small business ownership will have to do so at a much later start when compared to those who acquired business knowledge beforehand. Again, this is not to suggest that what was once lost is gone forever. Many people were successful and did not have the upbringing of entrepreneurial skills past down from one generation to the next. What is being suggested is that there is, and would be, an advantage to educating the youth about the benefits of entrepreneurship and owning a business to serve their community.

Not everyone has an equal opportunity to become an entrepreneur, as some must acquire a collection of basic skills, knowledge, and habits that may take decades to develop. Taking risks, working longer hours, and making critical decisions require a certain upbringing. Entrepreneurs are not created overnight but over time. However, ten years of working with a parent or an uncle as a youth, gaining practical knowledge, surely provides advantages later in life.

We cannot disregard the location and region in which we lived during the time of our early human capital acquisition. Being in one region versus another can surely impact our ability to develop a predisposition or insights needed for entrepreneurial behavior. We live in an area where several industries exist. Being surrounded by these industries allows us to either work for or start a business in a vein that is familiar to us. As with any location or local market, our human capital can be stymied in a region or location where a product or service is not valued or is not supported, although it might be highly valued in another market (i.e., if individuals have to take their product knowledge to another region where the consumers have higher subjective valuations of their productive goods or services).

Unfortunately, the opportunity to attain the same human capital at the same time and place that leads to entrepreneurship is not equally available to everyone.

Without the requisite human capital, one can only dream of becoming a successful entrepreneur or business owner. Families and family cultures vary across the globe, and so does the dissemination of knowledge at the family dinner table. We all come from backgrounds that either reward or punish certain behaviors that later transform into predispositions and values that underpin our ability to, at a minimum, think like and be an entrepreneur. Entrepreneurs "owe their position exclusively to the fact that they are a better fit for the performance of the functions incumbent upon them than other people are." [19] An interpretation of Mises on this point is that the required skills and knowledge develop over time to enable entrepreneurs to uniquely perform the production of products and services for the consumer.

---

[19] . L. von Mises, *Human Action* (Auburn, AL: Ludwig von Mises Institute, 1998).

Part 3

Routines, customs, traditions, and conventions are words
we use to note the persistence of informal constraints,
and it is the complex interaction of formal rules and
informal constraints, together with the way they are
enforced, that shapes our daily living and directs us
in the mundane activities that dominate our lives.

—Douglas North (1990)

Entrepreneurship (the action of creating novelty or investing
in economic developments), the innovator who brings forth
inventions for others to enjoy, and the people who start
ventures to afford them passive income, or those people who
by nature of other factors are forced into entrepreneurship,
look for signals to determine if saving and investing to a
degree is an act that will garner profits and not losses. What
is missing from the previous statement is the degree to which
rules and customs that guide entrepreneurs will determine
what profits and losses will ensue. Customs and traditions
embedded in institutions are so intertwined and affect the
judgment of entrepreneurs. Not to mention, judgment
is predicated on expectations—that is, expectations of

opportunities to be discovered and acted upon. There is no pretense here that tries to inflict upon customs, traditions, and beliefs as static; they are a set of guiding principles. Language, markets, money, and values are fundamental in how entrepreneurs at a cultural level interpret and build expectations of how and in which capacity they can use their knowledge, skills, or dormant talents to serve others and make a living for themselves. Culture is imbued with known behavior patterns; as a reframe, people do what they know and believe will provide them the best opportunity. Far from a deterministic view of culture, if included in this notion, the economy has business cycles that alter the flow and direction of consumer demand.

The business styles and responses speak to the notion that people import new cultural products, bring forth new knowledge, or, on the other hand, are forced by business cycles to use a dormant skill and knowledge to make or sell their resources in the marketplace. This dormant skill application to serve the consumer can happen via many marketplace mechanisms, including brick-and-mortar or e-platforms. Changes in the economy and in individuals' reactions align with the idea of a relentless character of entrepreneurship. Marketplace discoveries made by the entrepreneur do not come about via discussion of the best minds per se. Instead, most entrepreneurial discoveries are made in an unarticulated fashion and are imitated chiefly based on what others have done or are doing within their immediate purview, because if it worked for them in most cases, it works the same for other people. The institutions of entrepreneurial action available to potential and incumbent entrepreneurs are those that not only have been passed down in terms of available knowledge through the ages but are methods, ways of conduct, and values that, in short, are improvements or adjustments made by the actions of those who came before us. Entrepreneurs never start from scratch. They use the knowledge of others. Culture is an aspect of how entrepreneurial traditions play a vital part in how opportunities are interpreted and acted upon by real people.

12

Marketing and Advertising

This is certainly an exciting time, with many small and large companies making hasty decisions to cut back and, in many cases, to cut out of their budget, the most competitive market tool—advertising. Companies that are in survival mode should not decrease their advertising spend in the short run. It is an error to assume that customers are not searching for information about a product or service that you can provide. While on the surface it might seem clearheaded to eliminate marketing activities to protect your firm's assets, might we not forget that marketing in general and advertising are, in the end, informational devices that drive revenues for the long run? Everything has a cost, even information which increases customers' knowledge of what you offer, where, and at what price. Advertising identifies sellers to customers and reminds infrequent customers about changes in the state of the market. Companies change what they offer and at what price, along with the changes in customer consumption patterns. Therefore, marketing is an investment, not an expense—this especially rings true in a down economy.

Some say companies that consistently advertise reap significant market benefits more often than competing companies, even during a down economy. As far as advertising is concerned, marketing offers firms a market advantage when it comes to customer search costs and brand awareness in the long run. Decreasing marketing and advertising during a down economy comes at a cost to the company and the customer. Cutting advertising diminishes information in circulation, thereby cutting brand awareness, customer conversions, and unit sales. In a transitional economic landscape, firms that do not produce information (i.e., do not advertise and promote their products and services) increase customers' search costs. In a post-transitional economic landscape, those firms that decided to decrease marketing and advertising will have created an uphill battle for their firm, making it extremely difficult to break through the noise. If you want to be a market leader, understand that it costs to be the boss!

Marketing is information dissemination, and firms that do not promptly provide customers with useful information are sure to lose market share, awareness, and customer commitment. The loss of permanence and significance will be even more costly to a firm that does not advertise during a post-transitional economy, especially for nascent companies. Newer companies will suffer the long-run consequences of not advertising during a turning and adjusting economy. As opposed to established companies, nascent companies must break through established brand positions in the market.

Case in point, customers do not know what they need

to know unless you tell them—and trust me, they want to know! Without your firm's marketing, customers will be forced to search and purchase elsewhere. In other words, customers have *high time preferences*—they want satisfaction *now*—and added high search costs now will result in a more uncertain future for a company.

Now is the time to be even more vigilant about informing and educating your customers based on specific quality measures, prices, and your offering's importance to them. Remember, market success is about the delivery of timely, essential product or service information. Information delivery can be accomplished by incrementally informing customers via content pages, digital campaigns, podcasts, digital marketing, and digital promotions to reap the benefits of digital flexibility that increasingly lower customers' search costs.

We must also not forget that advertising is a social function, and one that should not be ignored but fulfilled. At the same time, advertising is the primary device in which companies of all types bring forth market opportunities to customers. That is, the information costs incurred by the customer are the driver from *not knowing* to *knowing*. Why would customers cease to accept information from their market providers during a down economy? Do customers cease buying things of importance during a down economy? Brands choosing to go dark on marketing must think about the subjective nature of customer value and expectations. Failing to meet expectations in the future will result in long periods of resuscitation going into a post-transitional economy.

There are many new methods on the horizon for you

to deliver timely advertising. However, it is best to use the technique most satisfactory to your customer, not to all customers (i.e., customers differ in the information they need). Deliver tailored information to your customers during this slowdown; this is a moment in time then much ground can be gained in lowering knowledge acquisition costs and increasing the rapid-fire production of information. During this down economy, continuous advertising enables customer conversions and, at any rate, reduces the information cost for customers who find themselves searching for updates of the state of the changing market.

Knowledge comes at a cost. Therefore, the mistake of not advertising will indeed allow a competitor to reap the benefits of your inaction. Unfortunately, customer information and decision-making often are based on past market conditions. Trust me; your customers will love you to keep them in mind, lower their search costs, and show your commitment to them when times are not so great.

Marketing as a set of communication devices is the single best tool to reach consumers far and near. However, marketing explained on the surface of things does not give it its full character and role in the matrix of entrepreneurs and consumer and capital markets. Marketing is a philosophy, a way to differentiate in many ways one firm from the next or one brand compared to the other brand. Differentiation is another way of claiming exclusive value offered to the consumer; it also explains the possible value claims. Marketing is the only tool in the entrepreneur's toolbox that can unravel abstract but clear consumer signals. Marketing is not just putting out (i.e., an output) but a feedback mechanism that closes the knowledge gap between market participants.

13

It's Not What Customers Say, It's What They Do

It is preposterous to assume that what customers say is more important than where they place their feet and the price they pay for products or services. The customer's mind is still elusive and challenging for entrepreneurs understand. If understanding the mind of the customer were easy, everyone would do it!

The insights of the Austrian school of economics tell us that people act purposefully toward future betterment. That is, customers and entrepreneurs both act to attain better future situations than their current situations compared to if they had not acted at all. Customers operate on a value scale, an important insight elucidating that value is in customers' minds. In this regard, it is best to "reduce the complex phenomena of human economic activity to the simplest elements." [20] For example, a recent article titled, "Two Simple Steps for Testing If Your First Customers Like Your Product," recommends conducting surveys and

---

[20] . C. Menger, *Principles of Economics* (Auburn, AL: Ludwig von Mises Institute, 2007).

searching for "moments of truth" and "tipping points." The only simple way of ascertaining customers' product sentiments is through the market itself.

The market process provides excellent insights into customers' unspoken motives and whether they like your products and services. The best way to figure out if your customers like your products is to turn to market phenomena. That is, the market price, as reflected by customers' subjective valuations and competitors' offerings. Different opinions about the value of a product or service are drawn out through this process. The real test, the market signals, shows how much and to what extent customers are willing to sacrifice to attain your product or service offering.

The customer wants the product with high use value, intended for whatever purposes to help them reach their end. The value of any product is in the customer's eye, the same way that beauty is in the beholder's eye! We never truly know to what extent a customer chooses your product over a competitor's. That is to say, the only reliable data on customer sentiments are that customers have purchased your products—the more, the merrier. Ludwig von Mises in *Human Action* expressed that, "It is ultimately always the subjective value judgments of individuals that determine the formation of prices." [21] Market prices and exchanges alert the entrepreneur whether the product is more or less valuable to the customer than the forgone opportunity to withhold their cash. Money measures prices, and prices measure value. Buying and selling or market abstention determine prices. As such, prices are what customers are willing to pay

---

[21] . *L. von Mises, Human Action (Auburn, AL: Ludwig von Mises Institute, 1998).*

for a product based on their subjective valuation, keeping in mind their future benefit from that product.

In his salient book, *Economics for Real People*, Gene Callahan agreed that "only real market prices convey information on the freely chosen values of acting man." [22]

Therefore, it is sensible to observe market price signals as a means of analyzing customer sentiments. Customer dissatisfaction and loyalty occur when product or service incongruities exist. Market incongruities also exist between the entrepreneur's perceptions of changing market realities. The entrepreneur's function is to address any market incongruities in which the customer, because of market changes, is better off than they were before. The market is in constant movement, which means customer preferences are in perpetual motion.

Retention of customers is a less complicated phenomenon that an entrepreneur might observe. Individuals act in concert with one another in a spontaneous way to reach their goals in any given market. As the author of the cited article proposes, the concept of customer retention is misguided because retention relates to competitors' actions and their substitutable products. The question should be, how many substitutable products exist in my ecosystem? Are other entrepreneurs doing the same that I am not doing?

First, the customer is the holder of the perception of value. Second, the customer making future choices is the cornerstone of the basic axiom of action. While taste preferences change over time, so do the market actions of your customers and your competitors. The first axiom of the

---

[22] . G. Callahan, *Economics for Real People* (Auburn, AL: Ludwig von Mises Institute, 2002).

order of the marketplace is that people act and make decisions based on limited bits of information; they act to pursue a better situation based on the choices they are presented with. Mises reminds us of this in his work titled *Human Action*. What the customer says and the actions customers take are two different things, because it is the customers' actions that provide market signals to the entrepreneur. If you satisfy the customers' needs and wants, profits will ensue and losses will decrease. You, the entrepreneur, strive to receive rewards for the risks involved in bringing new products to the market. Your competitors are seeking the same market rewards but in a reverse time frame.

Some do not understand how competition works as a signal of incongruities, leading to profits or losses. Indeed, competition exists so long as customers have market choices and can exercise them. The reality is that customers vote with their dollars and feet. They may voice their enjoyment of your products, but at the same time, are enthralled with a competitors' quality, service, and price of their product. Competition, therefore, acts as the entrepreneurs' lighthouse, guiding them toward market opportunities that may go unrealized or deterring them from those that are unfit.

Competition, in the Austrian view, is aimed at who can serve the customer best. Providing the best quality and product to the customer is the leading role of entrepreneurial competition. Competition is not and should not be insidious; rather, it should be productive and dynamic. If entrepreneur A wants to enter a market with capital to prove he or she can do things better than entrepreneur B, that should be his or her choice. Entrepreneur B will come to realize they missed many market opportunities only because that knowledge appears as a result of the competitiveness of entrepreneur A. For example, customers may choose the products of entrepreneur A one day and those of entrepreneur B the next.

It is not what customers say, but what they do. Entrepreneurial insight about the market and the changes that will occur should be the guiding light for entrepreneurs. Entrepreneurs must ascertain how people will respond to changes. Customer purchases, retention, a likeness of products or services, and loyalty are results of entrepreneurial market observation, and not causes.

14

Less Competition Means Less Consumer Happiness

We have heard people say that less is more. In the marketplace, more actually means more; and in some contexts, more is better. For example, more goods, more options, more ability paths, more e-platforms, more buyers, more sellers, and a variety of services. In *Essay on Economic Theory*, a manuscript written in 1730, Richard Cantillon said the following about the marketplace function of competition: "These entrepreneurs never know how great the demand will be in their city, nor how long their customers will buy from them since their rivals will try, by all sorts of means, to attract their customers." [23]

Consumer happiness is an individual sentiment based on the conversation between dissatisfaction and satisfaction. Happiness is relative and related to consumer factors such as price and income. What is the price of their most valued economic good and their relative income to expend on the economic good in question? Consumer happiness has better

---

[23] . R. Cantillon, *An Essay on Economic Theory* (Auburn, AL: Ludwig von Mises Institute, 2010).

results when firms can create better production methods and technology implementation to enhance consumer satisfaction for their most valued option. There is a direct relationship between consumer happiness and competition. What type of competition is more strongly related to happiness? Entrepreneurial firms might compete on the following bases in the marketplace to increase consumer happiness: sales, experiences, products, services, use of technology, brand awareness, and price. The antecedent of these effects is that effective technology speeds production or can develop the required capital to recombine resources to improve lagging production processes. I do not mean that all consumers' satisfaction will be fulfilled, as this is impossible because resources are scarce. Consumer dissatisfaction can be resolved when firms implement technological enhancements to their production process or inventions, or shift resources toward greater output in the direction of market demand that is more favorable than if causation was the reverse.

In many cases, consumer and business products may be substituted, which opens doors for competitors to use technology to lower the prices of goods. In regard to competition, we mean the freedom of entry and exit, substitutability, and originality to play itself out in the friction in the market adjustment process. The adjustment process is a sign of growth or something new that changes the direction and flow of production related to consumption. Therefore, "the process of growth in itself induces all sorts of unsymmetrical changes in the pattern of wants, of techniques, and the general level of consumption." [24]

No amount of production will solve dissatisfied

---

[24] . M. D. Wright, *Capitalism* (New York, NY: McGraw-Hill, 1951).

consumers, but we must realize that consumer search and value scales are predicated on a state of dissatisfaction. *Dissatisfaction* is the basis on which consumers seek out those consumer goods to meet their needs and wants. Typically, when thinking of consumer action, we consider how consumers are satisfied and do things to accomplish satisfaction. To understand consumer happiness, we must start with the causation of dissatisfaction. Being dissatisfied, where there is a void in wants or needs, is less discussed than consumer happiness and goal attainments. The dissatisfaction brings about market signals for entrepreneurs and manufacturers to resolve, which brings forth inventiveness and innovative products and services. There is, however, a connection between unobtained valued needs and wants, and that is that more competition implies a potential satisfied consumer population. Why do I assume this is the case? Companies that allow consumers to go unsatisfied and are making higher profits may be using a model that does not promote consumer satisfaction; they could be increasing their profits due to that reason. Again, the determination of profits is meaningful to the firm as to whether they are satisfied or have dissatisfied consumers.

It is amazing to see the reactions received when the word *competition* is brought up in a conversation regarding the conduction of business activity. I mean, isn't that what entrepreneurship, innovation, and exchange are all about? Kirzner told us that competition and the entrepreneur are functions of the marketplace. It appears there are two camps on competition: one is that all have perfect knowledge and no one firm can make a substantive difference in the price of goods in the market, and the other is from the Austrian school which views the foremost key as there being a semblance of freedom of entry.

As we get in our vehicle to drive to work, are we not competing with everyone else to get through the green light before the other drivers, to get into a place to eat breakfast, to find an empty parking spot closest to the building? Are we not in competition in the lunch line wherever we decide to dine? When looking for a job, applicants are in competition with other applicants for the same job. The reality is that some applicants will lose a spot in the employment race due to the competitive nature of employment transition. Whatever happened to *you win some and you lose some*? *Know when to hold them and know when to fold them.* Is that what I remembered? Nowadays, competition automatically turns heads; they think of an insidious form of competition. But what about emulation and imitation? The word competition means different things to different people.

Competition incentivizes suppliers and producers to meet the advancing needs of consumers. This type of competition is outside the scope of the antitrust paradox and is more in line with the production of consumer goods that have embedded costs savings because of technology, driving down costs for the consumer, not cutthroat *below the belt* fighting. We must understand under this pretext that a firm's profits are not at the expense of the consumer. Joel Dean said, "Most of the profits go to the more efficient suppliers, not the marginal supplier whose costly output is nonetheless required to satisfy the full demand at the prevailing market price." [25] Consumers willing to pay prices

[25] . B. B. Greaves, *Free Market Economics: A Basic Reader* (New York, NY: Irvington-on-Hudson, 1989).

for products and services must be paid enough not to use their skill sets in other more profitable marketplaces. In a sense, this conception of competition means that there will be unevenness in the entrepreneur's success or failure or profit and loss. Competing is a simple motivation and a tool. If done correctly and humanely, it can excel consumer offerings, thereby serving as a concrete signal via the marketplace to indirectly increase consumer well-being.

The problem is not creating an environment for firms to compete for consumers' well-being but the mindset of competing for everyday purposes. Whereas the common purpose of market participation is to enhance consumers' well-being, less competition means less consumer well-being. With that said, entrepreneurs do not have laser-focused vision to have the requisite foresight to know for certain if they have fully and successfully enhanced a consumer's well-being, except for one way—profits.

Profits are more than mere payment on the use of resources above costs; they are incentives for the producer, seller, or entrepreneur to keep doing the same thing: pursuing consumer wellness. No economic system will perfectly anticipate consumer values and future purchases, as growth and expansion affect different markets and industries differently. There is likely to be vested interests to be inconvenienced by competition and profit-making of the consistent movement of consumer needs and wants and the ability of competitors to cooperate by competing on price. Again, the vested interests are affected. Consider the following:

Cotton farmers would want to expand the output of oleomargarine; dairy farmers to prevent it. The West might want to build up new plants; the East might want to prevent it. Coal miners would object to hydroelectric plants; railroad workers and sailors to oil pipelines. [26]

Hence, the relentless pursuit of the market process and the effects of adjusting to consumer market responses are ongoing aspects of the market economy. The market process will notify a seller that there are other competitors in similar circumstances as the seller, and in some cases, there may be only one supplier or producer of a good. Both competitors and the entry of substitutable products will more than likely create a response involving the use of technology. Technology requires saving and investing by entrepreneurs, but not all technology is beneficial to consumer welfare—only what I call *good* technology.

Too often, there is loud noise around what technology is and is not as it relates to consumer satisfaction and use toward their ends. Instead, the focus here is not definitional but pertaining to marketplace use of technology and its effect on consumer satisfaction, wellness, and happiness. Technology is a critical element of the institution of entrepreneurship. Over many decades there have been predictions on the effects of various types of technologies on industries, production processes, and consumer products. How does technology that works and is responsive to consumer needs

---

[26] . M. D. Wright, *Capitalism* (New York, NY: McGraw-Hill Book Company, 1951).

lead to consumer happiness? While we are all recipients of technology—big or small—there is much that is overlooked (what I call good technology) which is neither high tech nor low tech but good tech.

Good tech has lasting power, solves problems, brings individuals happiness, and, when individuals apply good technology, fuels economic development. Good technology is relentless, useful, and leads individuals on the pursuit of their ultimate ends. It is a consistent pursuit of future innovation. Think about good technology this way: At the end of the day, we all use and apply some form of technology to accomplish our daily activities. Some use low tech, and some use high tech, but most human action uses good tech. What is good tech? When it comes to how we use technology, we might say *to each his own*; that is, we have our meaning for our use of technology in our daily lives. Technology is subjective. What works for me may not work for you, but we all employ technology. That is a given. But what is not given is the competitive forces and nonregulatory prescriptions that enable good technologies to have staying power and bubble to the top. Competitive open-market forces flush out the bad technology and bring good technology to the fore.

Good technology creates social networks, enables learning and human capital development, reshapes the way we think and act, pools our productive energies, and, entrepreneurially speaking, it has a profound positive effect on consumer happiness. Good technology improves consumer welfare; it does not degrade consumer welfare. Good technology enables the consumer to integrate. However, aside from consumer welfare, which is vital to a market economy, good technology can be and should be a mechanism to transform a non-entrepreneur into a mundane entrepreneur who transforms raw materials into final consumer goods—it is relentless in its long-run effects. Therefore, in the short run, bad tech is washed away by good competitive forces.

From a consumer's point of view, technology is comprised of advances in human action. You see, inadequate technology and good technology are neither big nor small but are relentless to allow people to do what they set out to achieve—education, passive income, investment tools, a career, or new production processes. Good technology allows people to be as productive as possible, enables consumers to pursue goals, and helps fuel good competitive market processes. Good technology is not solely the product or service but is the accumulative process between competitors through time. For instance, modern transportation, in and of itself, has transformed many times from biblical to modern times. Good technology will continue to persevere and find its best use in consumer business capital markets.

15

A Bird in the Hand Is Worth One in the Hand, Not Two in the Bush

As the old saying goes, a bird in the hand is worth two in the bush. But I wonder if the causation is the opposite: a bird in the hand is worth more than two in the bush. A bird in the hand is worth a bird in the hand when it comes to the timing that it would take to wait for a second bird to arrive in the bush at the expense of the bird already in hand. To be specific, in this case, we are referring to how entrepreneurs feel market gaps because of the needs and wants of consumers rather than the immediate consumption of their resources. The reality is that a bird in the hand is a bird in the hand. In many cases, the misunderstood function of the entrepreneur is how they close the marketplace gap on consumer time preferences. Eugen von Böhm-Bawerk laid out the explanation and rationale for time preference as a mechanism of rewarding the entrepreneur, rewarding the capitalists, and rewarding the consumer based on the available time frame. Consumers pursue value-seeking activities in the marketplace with short time horizons, and the entrepreneur has longer horizons.

Here I am referring to the high versus low time preferences as a differential between the entrepreneur and what they provide and when the consumer receives the economic goods demanded. The dovetailing concept of time preferences is hardly understood. Why? For example, someone looking to purchase a new vehicle may have an extremely high time preference if they need the vehicle as soon as possible to conduct their everyday activities. If the consumer has a higher time preference, the entrepreneur has a lower time preference. Lower and higher time preferences are neither good nor bad. As some say, it is what it is. I have a high time preference if I am looking for something that can solve my immediate needs. Conversely, the entrepreneur must save and use their savings to increase their productivity to meet market demand.

A society that can exercise time preferences has quite the advantage over societies that for whatever reason cannot, and sellers keep consumers waiting or add more time to the search costs for the consumer. This advantage goes unseen in terms of how a market economy works. More importantly, exchanging in subjective time preferences is an ingenious feature of an economic system. Think about if you, the consumer, have a low time preference, meaning you are willing to wait for a long time to purchase that vehicle that you need for daily activities. What would the world be like if consumers had a low time preference? As consumers, I daresay that our needs would mostly go unmet if entrepreneurial production, investment, and innovation were high time-preference ends. If entrepreneurs had a high time preference, rather than a low time preference, they would make market and investment errors due to the consumer's corresponding high time preferences. The entrepreneur with a low time preference allows the consuming society to acquire products and services in real time, not ten years later once the resources have been procured and finalized after the production process. It is the entrepreneur's low time preference that helps society meet individual goals via their personal investment and production.

A bird in the hand is worth a bird in the hand. Consumers want what they can have now, and not later. The entrepreneur must save for the time when consumers want the service or product at a future time.

> He who consumes a nonperishable good instead of postponing consumption for an indefinite later moment thereby reveals a higher valuation of present satisfaction as compared with later satisfaction. If he were not to prefer satisfaction in a nearer period of the future to that in a remoter period, he would never consume and so satisfy wants. He would not consume today, but he would not consume tomorrow either, as the morrow would confront him with the same alternative. [27]

Think about the high time preference of someone who needs an automobile to get back and forth to work

---

[27] . L. von Mises, *Human Action (Auburn, AL: Ludwig von Mises Institute, 1998).*

and for errands or for family transportation needs. The consumer does not have the time nor the need to figure the costs of finding the resources to manufacture a vehicle under typical time constraints. Consumers depend on the entrepreneurs to pick up market signals to invest capital in an acknowledged consumer need toward the production of the final consumer good—the automobile. For example, how would it be possible to go shopping for a vehicle, choose a vehicle that fits your expenses and style, pay for the vehicle, and drive it off the lot on the same day if time preferences were reversed? Better yet, how would it be possible to visit a vehicle seller's website and order the vehicle for pickup within a matter of hours if time preferences were reversed?

Broadly, economic goods are valued by consumers now. The same products or services are more relevant toward consumer ends; thereby, time preference rewards entrepreneurs for making profits by using superior forecasting of the needs of consumers within a specified time. A non-investing entrepreneur may notice they had a bicycle in their garage that has gone unused for some time, but the market signal has been noticed, and the owner decides that the bicycle can be used as capital for creating a delivery service. The entrepreneur anticipates there will not be enough of such products and services in a given marketplace at any given time; that is, they sense via prices and production whether there is enough production or service offerings to supply consumer demand. Benjamin Franklin said that haste makes waste, but entrepreneurially speaking, a bird in the hand is just as valuable as two in the bush.

A bird in the hand is worth more than two in the bush! In many cases, a present capital resource that has multiple purposes during changing situations is worth more than the expectation of a future use of the same capital resource. What would happen if the entrepreneur were wiped out of the economic picture? It would be almost impossible to wipe out the entrepreneur from the economic picture because society (you and me) value time, and we place a premium on it. The timing and the causes of preferences come into the picture with entrepreneurship and uncertainty, and consumer time preferences reward entrepreneurs for using or reusing supply in its intended or unintended combinations.

Not all consumers have high time preferences; some have low time preferences—they prefer to wait. Waiting is a consumer's prerogative. However, overall, the entrepreneur must, in many cases, have a lower time preference than consumers. What consumers prefer not to give up in their acquisition search is their expectations—"subjective wants with objective circumstances." [28]

The entrepreneur fills gaps in the market that relate to consumers' time and expectations, and filling them takes advantage of and directs profit opportunities and production of most urgently demanded resources. Unexpected changes in one's plans are the cause of new knowledge. The eminent Austrian economist, Ludwig Lachmann, added more clarity when he said, "Time cannot elapse without the state of knowledge changing. Decisions to act, by contrast, require a (temporarily) fixed state of knowledge to permit us to find our orientation in the position we happen to be in." Therefore, every time there is a change in future expectations, by contrast, there must be a change in plans even when it

---

[28] . L. M. Lachmann, *The Market as an Economic Process* (Oxford, UK: Blackwell Publishing, 1986).

changes time preferences of consumers' good acquisition and entrepreneurs' saving and investment strategies. As you can see, this is a short-run view of the entrepreneurial time preference, which makes this function of a market economy that much more complicated to discern. However, the choice is in the hands of the individual consumer, and entrepreneurial profit due to lower time preferences "occurs because there are persistent changes in market conditions." [29]

Thus, higher profits to the entrepreneur with low time preference show the entrepreneur's superior ability to fulfill consumer wants promptly. On the contrary, entrepreneurial losses due to inefficiency waste resources and fall into obscurity with other marginalized entrepreneurial attempts—never to be seen again. Marginalization of inefficient entrepreneurs is part of the cycle of business, be it a firm or a group of entrepreneurial people seeking to make something new or provide a service or business in their localized regions. Therefore, entrepreneurs and consumers alike are affected by the good use or misuse of capital. That is because not all capital is the same or a lump of assets. In other words, if capital is used incorrectly, it may lose its use value if it's not applied to production as its next best use or most profitable use in the short run. Entrepreneurs' capital is not a bundle of the exact same resources; they are all different pieces that have different values in how they are used to satisfy consumer demands.

Everyday people seeking to find an entrepreneurial path—be it via art, music, gaming programs, programming and coding, creating a new brand of clothing, making

---

[29] . T. C. Taylor, *An Introduction to Austrian Economics* (Auburn, AL: Ludwig von Mises Institute, 2008).

products out of their garage, or investing in economic development—are, in fact, lowering their time preferences based on potential consumer demand in the marketplace. For example, an entrepreneur who decides to use their heterogeneous resources to start a venture in streaming fitness classes is using their resources that have been held back from future use to meet the demands of perceived consumers. Resources withheld are based primarily on the entrepreneur anticipating those seeking to consume fitness products and services who have shorter time preferences of a streaming exercise class. Even the entrepreneur providing an exercise class via an online platform is, as time goes on, losing value in the resources for the exercise class. Along the same lines, an artist has resources that are not homogeneous; in fact, the artist's paint, brushes, sketch pads, and other supplies must be used in a timely fashion or they will lose their inherent value unless the artist is able to recombine them in real time. There again, in the cases of the entrepreneurial artist and the exercise coach, a bird in the hand is worth one in the bush.

16

Learning from the Marketplace

Entrepreneurs do not have infinite knowledge about the market. Entrepreneurs are not omniscient; they act to provide consumer value in the market before other entrepreneurs do. "Action therefore implies that man does not have omniscient knowledge." [30] If the entrepreneur were omniscient and had full knowledge, no change or action would be needed. New information and technological advancements are constantly happening, and people's perceptions and expectations are ever changing. Hence, firms need to adapt. In the process of adapting, they face competition. Entrepreneurial knowledge is gained through competition. Competition is the entrepreneur's teacher. Four ways in which competition becomes valuable are explored below.

Think about this: sports enthusiasts tune in to watch their favorite teams compete in an epic battle on the field. Fans eagerly watch the game to see who will win. Before the game, fans predict how the teams will use their advantages;

---

[30] . E. G. Dolan, *Praxeology: The Methodology of Austrian Economics* (Menlo Park, CA: Institute for Humane Studies, Inc., 1976).

they analyze players' statistics for skills and talents to be displayed. Each individual, of course, wants their team to beat the other team. Despite which team wins, fans are typically entertained. Additionally, both teams gain knowledge about the opposing team and learn better ways to win the next game. In sports, the better-performing team is encouraged to win! Why is there not the same enthusiasm in markets between firms? To me, there seems be a general paradoxical view as to the nature of competition.

The entrepreneur's knowledge expands as they interact with consumers and the price in which consumers are willing to pay for a product or service as compared to the alternatives in the marketplace. The market mechanism coordinates knowledge through a process where consumers reward specific businesses for certain knowledge. Entrepreneurs do not have a magic power or a crystal ball; they just do a better job of figuring out which knowledge will be rewarded. Then, they act on the knowledge that will be rewarded. This process happens if there is competition in the marketplace.

We know that real life and sports are different, but the point is that there are a few examples we can take from sports to show how and why competition provides knowledge to the entrepreneur. While some knowledge is costly and can rearrange firms in whole industries, without competition from newcomer entrepreneurial firms, the entrepreneur remains ignorant.

What exactly is competition? We might agree that it includes a general rivalry in a marketplace driven by market participants making decisions and judgments, and sellers outbidding each other for the consumer vote. We may also generally state that it is a consumer's act of buying one company's products and services in preference to another company's products and services. [31] A more mainstream assessment of competition can best be described as a situation where no one company can control a market.

The Austrian view of competition states that the market process is central to the adjustment of the ignorance entrepreneurs may have as to potential present or future selling prices suited to buyers and offerings that should or should not be pursued. The acknowledgment of the entrepreneur in the marketplace evokes competition and competitive actions. Therefore, to acknowledge the entrepreneur is to acknowledge competition. Israel Kirzner stated, "Entrepreneurship and competition are two sides of the same coin: that entrepreneurial activity is always competitive, and that competitive activity is always entrepreneurial." [32]

For instance, Dalsey, Hillblom, and Lynn (DHL)—the courier, parcel, and logistics firm—was the entrepreneurial newcomer to the logistics and mailing industry and found rough beginnings competing with existing firms. [33] They provided a healthy amount of competition to the established mail courier and parcel industries on a global scale that ultimately resulted in express services and consumer options that many enjoy today.

---

[31] . I. Kirzner, *Competition & Entrepreneurship* (Chicago, IL: University of Chicago Press, 1978). See this work for an Austrian perspective and definition of *competition*.

[32] . Kirzner, *Competition & Entrepreneurship*.

[33] . P. Chung and R. Bowie, *DHL: From Startup to Global Upstart* (Berlin: De Gruyter, 2017). This text describes the nature of coemption that existed from the firm's conception to the present day.

Uber, another example, dynamically challenged the taxi industry. Instead of calling a cab via telephone, they were innovative and employed an app service. Uber challenged the competition for labor and employed many people who otherwise felt it unnecessary or unable to enter the transport taxi industry. Another example is Airbnb. The entrepreneurial founders of Airbnb gained greater knowledge after creatively disrupting the hospitality industry.

Getting closer to the customer and gaining knowledge is how entrepreneurs find profit opportunities. For the entrepreneur, there are two kinds of knowledge acquisition: before-market knowledge and after-market knowledge. Entrepreneurs do not know *ex ante* all there is to know about a particular market and the likelihood of a service or product's profit potential; as well, entrepreneurs cannot know *ex post* if their service or product will receive consumers' votes. Regarding the entrepreneurial paradox of acquisition via competition, the adage rings true today: *you never hit the ball unless you go to bat.*

Ludwig von Mises stated, "We are historians of the future." [34] History is a series of complex events. The heterogeneity in knowledge makes it impossible to know everything there is to know about historic market trends, or markets outside of one's purview, for that matter. Friedrich von Hayek explained that there is no such thing as perfect knowledge among individuals at any given time among populations of people. Entrepreneurs know what is needed to serve consumers at a particular point in time under

---

[34] . L. von Mises, *Theory and History* (New Rochelle, NY: Arlington House Publishers, 1969). See this work to understand Mises's conception of the role of history related to markets.

specific market conditions. Perfect knowledge and a perfect forecast are inconceivable in the real world. Knowledge constantly changes. Even the places in which transmissions of knowledge occur change, too. In *Intellectuals and Society*, Thomas Sowell wrote, "The very land that people stand on is not the same in different places." [35] Entrepreneurs are not omniscient, nor are they omnipotent to change the course of the nature of time and place.

Competition is an ambiguous concept. It is viewed by existing entrepreneurs as a foe and by newcomer entrepreneurs as a friend. Depending on who is asked, you will get different responses. As the saying goes, *competition is good for you but not for me*—more competition for you, but less for me. Unfortunately, established firms see competition as an insidious force attacking it. But the reality is, new entrepreneurs sell products and offer services that an incumbent firm missed. A pure economic order is what Eugen von Böhm-Bawerk postulated would penetrate through artificial interference due to new market situations created. [36] If people are free to buy and sell in a marketplace, there will be competitors attempting to emulate a successful firm or pursue a current firm's missed profit opportunity.

There are numerous explanations for pursing market knowledge, none of which can be fully explained here. Two are at the top: (1) reward of profit as enticement to pursue

---

[35] . T. Sowell, *Intellectuals and Society* (New York, NY: Basic Books, 2016).

[36] . Eugen von Böhm-Bawerk, in *Control or Economic Law*, discusses the two categories of market power, as with interference the market power is thus ineffective for periods of time.

market knowledge and (2) observing others' successes and attempting to replicate those successes.

Since the market is riddled with emerging firms that sense they can do what your firm does and better, new knowledge will be generated. The acquisition of new market knowledge is a means to a particular end: action. New knowledge supersedes old knowledge. But there is no surety that knowledge will be obsolete tomorrow, according to Ludwig Lachmann. [37]

There is always a way to do things better, with greater quality, and at a lower price. Market competition is a process of discovery and innovation. Incumbent firms, who once had an advantage, may not share in the enthusiasm of innovative practices being employed in their own backyard. Fernando Monteiro D'Andrea stated, "Firms that hold competitive advantages will have to defend their position by innovating continuously because competitors will act to try to overcome the other firm's competitive advantage through the modification of their own set of resources." [38] This is the hallmark of the Austrian school. D'Andrea illuminates the true nature of being an entrepreneur and the paradoxical view that exists regarding the function of competition.

For instance, established firms view competition as a foe because there will always be newcomer entrepreneurial firms that are more flexible and responsive to shifts in consumer

---

[37] . Ludwig Lachmann, in *The Foundations of Modern Austrian Economics*, in the chapter titled "On the Central Concept of Austrian Economics: Market Process," addressed the role of the entrepreneur and the market competitiveness, mainly how knowledge is spun out of these two market factors.

[38] . M. F. D'Andrea, *7 Lessons Business Owners Can Learn from Austrian Economics* (Auburn, AL: Mises Wire, 2018).

taste and are willing to supply new demand. Newcomer firms are quick to use inventions to enhance their offerings that are of better quality and at a better price relative to the incumbent firm. Entrepreneurs must realize that competition drives knowledge. Thus, as competitors interact with one another and with consumers, new knowledge is created.

Entrepreneurs who do not participant in the economic world will remain ignorant of new market data. By collecting data, experiencing market changes, and acquiring feedback from participants, entrepreneurs break out of a state of ignorance and become more knowledgeable of consumer needs and market demands. It is amazing how quickly inertia sets in when there are no competitors in a market. Healthy competition signals to entrepreneurs what not to pursue and what is advantageous to pursue. As the saying goes, iron sharpens iron. Only in the case where there is free entry to markets do entrepreneurs attain knowledge. Competition induces voluntary interaction between market entrepreneurs and the results of consumers' decision-making. This is noncoercive, unhampered interaction between people. As decision makers interact in the marketplace, they discover opportunities for what is and what can be. This is a given to any entrepreneur. Kirzner contended that competitive pressure is part of the character of the market; we can never be disentangled from it. If a profitable service or product is found or created, others can and will imitate the success and share in the profits. Most of the time, entrepreneurial pursuits can be imitated. Measuring the gains and profits resulting from competition is elusive and difficult to ascertain.

The key is to understand and use the healthy aspects of competition. Competition is the *perennial gale* of the market process and facilitates the propensity of the entrepreneur's ability to creatively disrupt markets, which includes vying for products and services that are new and altering the way industry rivals reconfigure and recombine their resources, as Schumpeter said. That is, the entrepreneur creatively seeks niche and uncontested markets with potential profit opportunities when rivalry is high. The entrepreneurial competitive element is helpful when entrepreneurs attempt to discover better methods than what has been done before and in uncontested markets where resources can be readily applied to new market participants.

Existing firms often shun real-world competition. Setting the market process in motion starts with the entrepreneur coming out of a state of market ignorance about the opportunities and prices of goods based on consumer decisions. This level of knowledge only arises via competition. This vital knowledge helps entrepreneurs enter markets to serve consumers, and that is guided by consumers' time preferences and their subjective valuations between competitors' goods. You would be hard pressed to hear an existing firm state that competition will make them better off, or that competition will teach them about the changes in the market, or that competition will make the consumer better off. There are forces that keep new competitors from entering markets. According to Mises, entrepreneurs are in competition for attaining means and a share in market success. [39] The bottom line is that market competition is not bad. It is an inherent part of the process where entrepreneurs seek to acquire knowledge, knowing that they are far from omniscient in market knowledge and never will be, if knowledge is omnipotent and omnipresent as a result of uncoercive, unhampered free competition.

---

[39] . L. von Mises, *The Free Market and Its Enemies: Pseudo-Science, Socialism, and Inflation* (New York, NY: Foundation for Economic Education, 2004).

17

Society's Entrepreneurial Engine

Although there is a proliferation of goods and services brought to markets by entrepreneurially minded producers and investors, the amount of production that is operative today was preceded by someone or some firm that harnessed the power of human capital in the past in order to produce those goods and services.

Unfortunately, this is often ignored. Instead, we are regularly confronted by arguments against markets and against the value of entrepreneurs. This often involves attacks on the very attitudes that lead to entrepreneurship itself. Over time, these attitudes kill the spirit of entrepreneurship and stymie growth potential. Promoting this *negative human capital* works against the vital consumer-entrepreneur market process. Who will serve the consumer? Negative human capital slows the engine of entrepreneurship and does not cultivate human flourishing. The view is that the market as a process is always a determining factor in entrepreneurial activity where people operate and must make decisions.

In *Wealth, Poverty, and Politics*, Thomas Sowell wrote,

"Transferring the fruits of human capital is not as fundamental as spreading the human capital itself." [40] Negative human capital is characterized as a nonproductive attitude without alertness to market demands, differences toward learning new skill sets, producing value for someone else, or the disdain for the mundane knowledge. A simple phrase captures the essence of negative human capital: "Someone else will make it, so I don't have to," or, "If customers do not buy my product or service, my business has failed." These statements represent one perspective of negative human capital. Another might be cultural impediments toward learning different ideas or skills from other people outside one's own cultural group, how individuals within a cultural group invest their time toward the replacement or acquisition of a new trade or market discovery, and one's willingness to serve the customer. If entrepreneurship is dwindling in terms of growth potential over time, as some have reported, the dwindling factor might be the negative human capital that is diffused through many peoples and cultures. These inherently negative attitudes about human capital that many possess are aimed at, among other things, the values, habits, and skills needed for self-ownership and economic freedom. It is one thing to buy a product or acquire a service, it is another altogether to produce it.

The fact of the matter is, these broad factors may not show up in analyses, but they have detrimental effects, producing a negative view of self-ownership and the skills needed to engage in the market, not only for consumption but for the imperative of production, as this is how early Americans

---

[40] . T. Sowell, *Wealth, Poverty and Politics* (New York, NY. Basic Books, 2016).

survived. Daily, entrepreneurs encounter inherent market and cultural impediments that function as constraints and that do not show up on models and statistical projections.

A negative attitude about the skills needed for economic freedom reduces the enterprising spirit. These differences in attitudes and habits cannot be measured by a statistical box score analysis but are nonetheless evident in outcomes. Negative human capital is transmitted and carries with it thoughts such as, "If it ain't broke, don't fix it," or, "Someone else will produce it and bring it to market." There are many reasons why families, cultures, nations, and individuals disdain the acquisition of market human capital while some take advantage of and embrace the acquisition of market-based skills.

Real entrepreneurs must make decisions and judgments about what they can do and what they cannot do to operate a business. These are affected by internal and external cultural impediments and attitudes toward changing market circumstances that require investments and flexibility in acquiring or borrowing human capital from others. Sowell noted the cultural constraints of negative human capital in terms of skills: "A nation whose population remained illiterate, while literacy became widespread among other nations, will of course benefit from people on par with people in countries where literacy has been the norm for generations, or for centuries." [41]

For instance, the Chinese of the sixteenth and seventeenth centuries valued skills in time and astrology. Although Western nations had introduced them to the clock, it remained a curious toy at the time. In addition to beliefs

---

[41] . T. Sowell, *Wealth, Poverty and Politics*.

and values attached to skills and mobility of said skills, human capital is a nation's most vital asset for successful entrepreneurship and economic vitality. For example, during the sixteenth century, France profited from skilled Italian craftsmen. After the sixteenth century, when the Italian craftsmen had greater mobility and were no longer tied to French markets, France lost numerous workers who could not readily be replaced.

Attitudes differ between those who start businesses and those who do not. Let us be honest, some have negative attitudes toward what constitutes work or production at work. Even a person's career choice is intricately tied to one's attitude about the investment in or acquisition of human capital and the benefits that can be obtained with it in the market. Those with positive attitudes regarding their self-development and acquired skills invest so that they can reap economic benefits and serve others. These investments consist of learning new things, adapting to different challenges, living through various circumstances, and experiencing life and learning from others. Why would entrepreneurship be any different? Negative attitudes toward human capital development are detrimental to the future of entrepreneurship and to economic prosperity.

There are numerous ways to gain human capital that can be rewarded in the marketplace, stemming from experience on the job, hobbies, educational classes, and new learning experiences. *Consuming* goods and services does not take the place of *learning* how those goods and services are produced. Entrepreneurship and its advancement are affected by individuals who disdain the notion of commercial and industrial enterprise, self-ownership, private property, and the benefits of freedom of exchange. Surely, if families and social circles provide products and services without investing in tacit learning and seeking economic freedom with that tacit knowledge, there will be increasingly less growth and long-run prosperity for entrepreneurs.

What or who is to blame for negative views of self-ownership? Can we suppose that at the cultural level some are more apt to invest in the knowledge and experience needed to build up one's human capital advantage, or that in other cultures assets are unable to be realized and opportunities to realize them are sparse? It is amazing how, within various cultural groups, there are individuals who, no matter where they go, will find market gaps and fill them for the general population of consumers. How is it that some persist in production and self-ownership while others do not? It is simple: there is a negative attitude toward the human capital needed to acquire economic freedom.

18

An Unevenly Distributed World

We live in an unevenly distributed world. *No two things are alike* is the old saying. This saying has credence in the past, in our current time, and for the future. Why? Value judgments between two people on the same item will not be the same or, in some cases, even remotely similar. Case in point, knowledge and productivity are unevenly distributed among people and cultures. What is peculiar to me is the supposition that all or most things should be evenly distributed—including resources. The only thing that may be evenly distributed is the potentiality of one's actions. An unevenness of the world exists, and it exists even if society tries to manually even it out. Since we do know that knowledge and skills are not mutually exclusive, it implies that there is someone who will be willing to exchange one thing for another to reward the individual for the use of their skills.

Take football as an example. If football intelligence and skills were evenly distributed, we could all quarterback in the likes of Tom Brady or Russell Wilson and catch those unbelievable passes thrown to wide receivers like Randy Moss and Tyreek Hill. Even wealth created by entrepreneurs serving others for the continuation of a business has shown through acquisitions, mergers, and bankruptcies that success is unevenly distributed. Whatever the case, it is the unevenly distributed world that allows dedication, commitment, and positive attitude toward a work ethic to pay off.

Take, for example, the convention of the consumer—the amalgamation of people with similar characteristics, needs, and wants who have for so long been assumed to use the same methods to seek value. This consumer convention is more profound than we assume on the face of it. These consumer conventions are what sellers have so long assumed are the best methods to attract potential buyers and consumers via a value proposition. Even the notion of advertising to particular segments or groupings of customers with similar characteristics gives a false impression that intergroup characteristics are closely related between the vast differences in consumers in value-seeking patterns. This assumption furthermore implies that customers have the same knowledge and can use said knowledge simultaneously. Not to mention, customers' experiences are vastly different in time and place.

Knowledge leading to technological advancements is one of the most unevenly distributed goods known to man. If you could ask Queen Elizabeth, who reigned during the fifteenth century, if knowledge is unevenly distributed, she would agree. The reign of the Elizabethan time resulted from many cultures transmitting knowledge that lent itself to the greater prosperity of her kingdom. The knowledge that the Italians, the Spanish, and the Portuguese had in fabric-making contributed mightily to European commerce and transportation technology. Francis Bacon spoke of inventions and discoveries of his time. He elaborated on the fruitful development of Europe as a result, and its effects on Europe and the world on later innovations:

> It is well to observe the force and virtue and consequences of discoveries. These are to be nowhere seen more conspicuously than in those three which were unknown to the ancients, and of which the origin, though recent, is obscure and inglorious; namely, printing, gunpowder, and the magnet. [42]

Francis Bacon understood well the importance of discovery, commerce, trade, and ideas. What stumped him is the effect of time; he did not notice the rapid development of technology and its accumulation over time. Plato may have referred to what Bacon alluded to as the spirit of change. Time as a function of how people act is also one of those uneven facts of life. Just imagine if everyone in society operated on their goals at the same time—either in the short term or the long term—there would be no room to save or spend to exchange with other people. Some people want things sooner, and some want things later. Production takes time; this time is a factor of production for which the consumer is willing to wait to buy and the producer is eager to sell.

The institutions of economic systems serve as light posts

---

[42] . M. Edwards, *East-West Passage* (New York: Taplinger Publishing Company, 1971).

that illuminate people's creativity, which is vastly important for the multitude of people to make decisions—that is, to understand the effects of a decision (to buy or sell) and the consequences. The single notion that entrepreneurs' creativity is the primary requisite to marketplace entry is vital, but again, still an uneven characteristic. To qualify this point, it is possible that everyone can be creative, but the incentive to be creative is still unevenly distributed throughout society. Sometimes it is easy to overcomplicate and undervalue the ways in which an economy ought to operate under equal conditions. What is needed for a consumer to make a purchasing decision and for the entrepreneur to provide the item of consumption at a particular location for the consumer to buy? Ask the average person: what insights do individuals need in order to understand what happens in an economy in terms of what is needed to make an exchange? Odds are, that person will say that consumers seek to buy things and entrepreneurs seek to sell things. So, what creates this wave-like unevenness in the marketplace?

Sir William Petty, a seventeenth-century English philosopher, is the writer whose ideas paved the way for the development of the concept called the division of labor. Later, Adam Smith, an eighteenth-century Scottish philosopher and economist who wrote *The Wealth of Nations*, elaborated on the functions and reasoning behind a division of labor. Smith used the pin shop as an exemplar for the workings of the division of labor. Fast forward to the present time, and the division of labor is used as a means directed with technological advances, global networks, training, and digital infrastructure—an infrastructure that enables firms and entrepreneurs to produce and invest in broader areas of society.

A division of labor also creates for the consumer greater satisfaction and better service options. The reason for this is quite simple. The marketplace can be seen as a perpetual election, where the returns determine which business should remain in operation and which should leave the marketplace. Given the imperative of creating and producing for consumption and value acquisition, technology enables unknown entrepreneurs to join the marketplace in unconventional methods. The institution of competition optimizes a division of labor that provides independent opportunities for entrepreneurs. Market *spaces* and market*places* welcome swaths of everyday people to join social platforms to buy and sell economic goods, but to a larger degree. We might call this transition of entrepreneurial place to space *digitizing entrepreneurship*. In many respects, the division of labor is seen as a profession where tasks are separated and partitioned, thereby creating specialization. Benefits of the division of labor of entrepreneurship are greater innovation on the part of the entrepreneur, lower prices, consumer happiness, productivity, and economic allocation of human capital for this social function.

Let's take, for example, the breakdown of a process and the tools of production to allow for greater efficiencies and inventions. With the advent of technological improvements in production, there are two camps when it comes to the application of automation and its effect on human labor in the workplace. Automation is completing the tasks and producing in business sectors the way in which humans did sometime in the past. Critics of innovation related to automating productive tasks suggest that new productive processes will eliminate jobs that you and I have or had; others believe the increasing technological methods automating work will open up more opportunities for the application of human capital. Think about this: the cashier was a pivotal person in the retail sector, and the waiter or hostess was critical in the restaurant industry. The once-prized retailer, as we have seen of late, is slowly moving to the outskirts of business. Distributors see that going to the consumer may have more advantages than going through the retailer. Fully automated processes are enabling more breakthroughs in innovations and discoveries. The fully automated fast-food kitchens to serve consumers will create unevenness in the quick-service industry, no doubt.

What are the long-term effects of automating the firm? There are two camps regarding what happens in the firm and its relation to what happens outside of the firm, objectively and subjectively speaking. One of the most significant obstacles that any firm in any economy faces is the malinvestment of scare resources in an ever-changing market economy. It is difficult or impossible to ascertain the future. Firms are faced with objective circumstances and subjective means. Formulating unique ways to employ scarce resources to reap a return on such resources has been answered predominately by theorists with a *static view* of the world. Unforeseen market changes pose problems with static strategic formulation methods and ultimate pursuits. Additionally, a firm's resources are not the same; they are heterogeneous in their use and application toward the output of the firm. Resources within a firm are unevenly used toward business goals. The spontaneous consumer changes, the investor, and entrepreneurship in relation to innovation occur at different times and at different rates that often do not move in lockstep. The idea of business strategy at its current conceptualization does not match the new era of market demands. Where can we find an even distribution of anything in the marketplace?

19

The Rise of the Digital Hand and the Emerging Class of Digitalpreneurs

In *An Inquiry into the Nature and Causes of the Wealth of Nations*, [43] Adam Smith described what he called the Invisible Hand, a metaphor to describe the mechanism of the market and the social benefit that individuals who participate in the market in self-interested ways intentionally and unintentionally serve others. The invisible hand guides individuals entrepreneurially to improve their own circumstances, and they unintentionally or unconsciously create social benefits for everyone by serving the ultimate purpose of creating markets, economic growth, trade, and prosperity. The invisible hand guides individuals' purposes to the most needed ends—the benefit that customers value most highly—and they express these purposes by using their skills and resources in market pursuits that benefit the larger society, intended or otherwise.

---

[43] . A. Smith, *An Inquiry into the Nature and Causes of Wealth of Nations* (Indianapolis, IN: Liberty Fund, 1776).

Alfred Chandler, on the contrary, took the opposite approach and described the *visible hand,* which he said was a managerial revolution. The *visible hand* guided the managerial class of large enterprises and replaced the spontaneous order of the *invisible hand* with the *visible hand* of experts managing production, focusing on mass manufacturing and distribution. Alfred Chandler said, "Such internalization permitted the *Visible Hand* of administrative coordination to make more intensive use of resources invested in these processes of production and distribution than could the *Invisible Hand* of market coordination." [44] Chandler sought to replace the implicit guidance of the *invisible hand* with the explicit control of an elite management class and the tools of organizational structure, command and control methods, and tightly constructed processes.

We are seeing the results of the *visible hand* today, in the rigid structures of established businesses that struggle to respond to fast-paced change and rapid innovation, and in the rejection of business by younger generations who see it as elitist and exploitative. Happily, the *visible hand* is losing its grip. Today, what I see emerging is the *digital hand.*

---

[44] . A. D. Chandler Jr., *The Visible Hand* (Cambridge, MA: Harvard University Press, 2002).

Table 1: Descriptions and Characteristics of The Market Hands

Independent individual acts aimed at bettering one's own circumstances result in general betterment for society
- Unarticulated guidance
- Spontaneous order
- Free markets
- Slow trickle-down lag in social benefits

Expert imposed management, structure and process required for the scale and complexity of mass production.
Expert guidance
Managed order
Mixed markets
High barrier of entry
Concentrated benefits to management class

Resources and infrastructure are made more broadly accessible so that anyone can be an entrepreneur and start, run and sustain a business.
- Mass accessibility
- Wisdom of crowds
- Digital guidance
- Low start-up costs
- Low barrier of entry
- Direct and immediate individual and social benefits

As Table 1 indicates, the digital hand is the enablement of a broad and deep population of new entrepreneurs who have easy access to infrastructure and resources available via the Internet and who can connect to every available source of knowledge, expertise, and support. The digital hand opens economic opportunities for everyday people who can participate as entrepreneurs in today's economic market spaces. E-commerce and digital market spaces are giving rise to digitalpreneurs, both nationally and globally. Chandler's *visible hand* has made significant improvements in the production of economic goods and mass service offerings, no doubt. However, never in human history has there been a digital hand guiding individuals who offer services, products, and entertainment with the power of prosperity, except in this current time of mass accessibility of e-commerce platforms.

Recent data suggests that social e-platforms, digital stores, and online market spaces are a $200 billion industry. The cause of this boon is the result of *human action* and not of *human design; the effect is the opportunity for regular people—not Chandler's elite—to be guided to economic success by the digital hand*. Now brick-and-mortar business models can be offered through a digital market space or a hybrid of both: click-and-mortar. One-person start-ups, small teams, or small- and medium-sized businesses can harness the virtually unlimited resources of the digitally interconnected global economy and serve its digitally interconnected markets.

Is the entrepreneurial participation of everyday people using digital platforms via the digital hand the final, irreversible shift to free and unhampered markets? Is the level of ease for the average person to be involved in the market process the great breakthrough for individual economic freedom, even though their investment in entrepreneurial endeavors is not as consequential as an investment of a high-profile millionaire or billionaire? In the short run, we see more real people—you, your neighbors, and your friends—profitably exercising their talents, serving consumers, and using the digital hand. In the long run, an entire emergent class of individuals can realize their positive impact on society using the digital hand.

With a tremendous uptick in digital business opportunities within the past decade, there is anticipation that more digitalpreneurs will arise in the future, thereby expanding this class of entrepreneurs. Facebook's Marketplace has grown to millions of sellers across many countries, providing real people with enormous entrepreneurial and innovative opportunities within just a few years of its formation in the digital space. No matter the *division of labor* one represents in the e-commerce sphere, there are sufficient and inexpensive market spaces to enable the expression of entrepreneurship. Poshmark, eBay, Etsy, Shopify, Volusion, and other e-commerce market spaces have built-in buyer networks serving millions of people. These e-platforms remove arbitrary barriers to the advancement of everyday people who wish to participate in the market space. Digitalpreneurs, newcomers, or entrepreneurs transitioning to digital platforms develop entrepreneurial skills and can profit from them.

Additionally, digitalpreneurs have noticeable positive effects on value creation for customers and motivation for sellers. Value in a subjective sense can exchange for digitalpreneurs' presented value. Digitalpreneurs provide a subjectively valued service, and in response, the value is immediately returned to the digitalpreneur based on the service obtained by the consumer. The consumer pays the digitalpreneur according to the value of the service received. The *digital hand*, like the i*nvisible hand*, rewards people who are efficient in filling market gaps. Unlike the *visible hand*, the digital hand uses the knowledge and experiences of many, which is what F. A. Hayek called dispersed knowledge, so that value can only be exchanged for what it is perceived in worth. The upside to the digital hand is that there is always something for somebody in the vast market space.

Therefore, the effect of open market spaces is the emergence of an entrepreneurial class who are nimble and fast-acting by their very nature. The class of digitalpreneurs individualizes market-space levels of participation across diversified products and services, or both.

Ultimately, e-platforms and digital market spaces are creating a process whereby real people with various levels of investment in the economy can do good. How long will this last? While the youngster creating skateboards to sell on social market spaces and digital apps is not investing at the amounts of an Elon Musk or Daymond John, he or she is nevertheless engaging in entrepreneurship using the digital hand. The retired musician can use the digital hand to stream music lessons to people who live thousands of miles away or to someone next door. Up-and-coming musicians may not sell as many records as Bruno Mars, Carrie Underwood, or Rihanna but they can be heard across various countries by listeners and admirers with one swipe across the smartphone screen. The aspiring musician can receive the face value of their streaming services. Using resources, serving consumers while making a profit, saving, reinvesting, and future growth—isn't this what entrepreneurship is about? With the digital hand, producers can produce more, and consumers can choose from far more options by rising producers or artists who choose to use their superior offerings and talents to contribute to society's workings.

The digital hand in the short run ought to increase individuals' entrepreneurial freedom, thereby creating an emerging class. In this regard, I think Ludwig von Mises said it best: "The meaning of economic freedom is this: that the individual is in a position to choose the way in which he wants to integrate himself into the totality of society." There are positive short- and long-run effects emanating from this digital class of entrepreneurs that are yet to be seen.

20

Are Digital Market Spaces the Last Free-Market Frontier?

In his book, *The Theory of Moral Sentiments*, Adam Smith said of producers: "They are led by an invisible hand to make nearly the same distribution of the necessaries of life which would have been made had the earth been divided into equal portions among all inhabitants; and thus, without intending it, without knowing it, advance the interest of society, and afford means to the multiplication of the species." [45] As an institution of entrepreneurship, the digital market space is the modern version of Smith's invisible hand: a complex phenomenon that has not been designed by any one person but has emerged as a result of the usefulness that it provides to individuals in pursuing their goals by serving other market-space participants through value-providing exchanges.

These value-providing economic participants are people who are not highly capitalized, not holders of special permits, and have not paid large sums in start-up fees. Many are

---

[45] . A. Smith, *The Theory of Moral Sentiments* (New Rochelle, NY: Arlington House, 2010).

retirees, stay-at-home parents, or young adults who want to start small. All of them have much to gain from the advent of the digital market space. They are everyday entrepreneurs who are prospering in unprecedented ways via the market space.

Today, more than ever before, everyday entrepreneurs are using e-commerce and social platforms because they have lower barriers to entry, comparatively lower start-up costs, minimum fees, and in many cases, no costly permits. We know it to be universally true that fees, permits, licenses, and undue barriers automatically write a portion of the population out of the economic picture. Not to mention the growing e-commerce trends are reflecting changes in individual habits along with shifts in social conventions:

1. Compared with the brick-and-mortar marketplace model, the digital market space demonstrates the explicit rationale for why everyday people choose the digital hand: ease of entry into entrepreneurship.
2. The digital hand allows mutually beneficial exchanges to happen and relative freedom of access to often closed or uncontested markets.
3. The digital hand guides digitalpreneurs to apply their resources to the best use in the market space.
4. The market space rewards individual purposeful action and provides the incentive for individual discovery opportunities.

The digital hand is the proximate cause of millions of people entering the emerging digitalpreneurs class—those who sell products and services via e-platforms on digital devices. The dead hand, in contrast, is an emerging anti-market hand. The dead hand imposes a heavy counterweight effect by its interventionist, anti-market, anti-innovative policies that adversely affect the rising class of digitalpreneurs in the long run. The dead hand tends toward intervention; increasing regulatory requirements, requiring large amounts of start-up capital, and imposing licensing requirements and other fees of entry that hamper the positive effect of digitalpreneurship for everyday people. Unlike the digital hand, the dead hand does not create wealth or create value; it seizes resources and eliminates wealth creation, and it does so by disallowing individual privately held resources to be employed in higher uses in the market space. The dead hand disrupts the fundamental entrepreneurial institutions of private ownership and freedom of exchange.

The dead hand intends to intervene in a growing and prosperous economic process with policies and regulations that have good intentions but adverse effects on this rising class of people. Just think, the resale market is expected to reach $30 billion by 2030, according to Allison Prang of the *Wall Street Journal*. Imagine a free space in the market where people who do not have millions of dollars in seed money, capital equipment, or a storefront with overhead costs can enter a market space and serve others and themselves. They may be collectors who later decide to resell their collection, or they may be individual creators of products (creating it yourself, or CIY) of their art, music, crafted furniture, etc. The dead hand does not peer beyond the tangible, measurable, and visible effects of an individual's ability to engage and prosper in the market space. It does not recognize the opulence of the invisible effects of peaceful, energetic, and voluntary exchanges that are bettering life circumstances for many individuals in the pursuit of their purpose.

The dead hand may be getting stronger. Recently, a proliferation of restraints and regulations have been imposed on marketplace sellers on social and e-commerce platforms. The dead hand seeks to assert itself against the last free-market frontier. The dead hand may be a well-meaning hand, but its force has unintended effects. Case in point, brick-and-mortar is unattainable for some and has become marginalized by the pandemic, and start-up costs and barriers are high. Brick-and-mortar still has its place, but digital market spaces are growing at an astronomical rate. In perspective, e-commerce had approximately 2.1 billion digital buyers in 2020. The rise of the dead hand will destroy this last frontier where everyday people can flourish via the economic process.

We have to ask whether e-commerce and social platforms will remain free and unhampered in the long run. In the long run, will everyday entrepreneurs (i.e., stay-at-home parents, work-from-home contractors, retirees, and young adults) employ digital means to participate in the economic process? In other words, will the dead hand discourage people from using their resources to produce a product or offer a superior service, thereby making either a profit or a loss in market spaces? If they profit, will they be able to save and reinvest their profit back into the business, or will the dead hand take it away? Or will the dead hand make saving impossible by charging higher fees, taxes, and associated permits? The dead hand seeks to raise the barriers to market spaces and costs associated with e-commerce and digital platforms, making it an unattractive option for many who do not have the millions of dollars in financial capital to pursue entrepreneurial opportunities under the traditional brick-and-mortar business model.

We face a potential conflict. There is a rising class of digitalpreneurs and a rising dead hand that seeks to impose restrictions on them. The appeal of the digital hand is that it opens up entry barriers for everyday people to prosper in the economic processes. What would hold any entrepreneur back from the utilization of this free entry? Only the dead hand that restricts market entry. Put into the larger context, the dead hand, if you will, does not ensure socially discovered opportunities held privately by individuals. The dead hand alters individual purposeful action, which guides individuals to optimal courses of action when discoveries are apparent.

Well, it has been said that all good things come to an end; hopefully, market spaces will remain a good option for people as an entry into the entrepreneurial process, but the indicator of current trends suggests that the dead hand could be dominant sooner rather than later, and it will lay down a heavy hand on market spaces, which will have unintended consequences for digitalpreneurs. The trends include controls and regulations that are unnecessarily restrictive to everyday people in the real world. Limits imposed by the dead hand are overt and make it impossible to use the market to enter the economic process.

Fortunately, for some who represent the growing portion of the millions of individuals using the digital hand in the market space, they have reaped benefits from the digital hand. Real people serving online consumers have a significant ripple effect outside of the consumer market.

The everyday digitalpreneur is part of the increased revenue and profitability for many industries in the form of drop-shipping services, mobile shopping, and transportation and logistics.

Howard Baetjer Jr., in his book, *Economics and Free Markets,* asked, "Should competent adults be allowed to exchange freely with one another?" [46] I assert that we all agree, yes. The dead hand restricts freedom of exchange with an individual's property and services on "mutually agreeable" terms. The digital market space operates so that the average person can rise in society through the acquisition and disposition of privately held resources, talents, and skills that have value to other digital buyers sold at a price deemed sufficient by the buyers.

Is the digital hand the last frontier for the average person to do good business in market spaces? The problem with the dead hand is that it imposes barriers that eliminate the incentive for many to consider selling on eBay, Etsy, Poshmark, etc. A requirement for permits and upfront fees to start entrepreneurial activities will impose disincentives to conduct business in market spaces. Why? F.A. Hayek said to this point,

> It would seem that a rational economic policy should confine itself to creating the conditions in which the market will function as well as possible, but should not regard it as its task to influence or guide the individual activities.

---

[46] . H. Baetjer Jr., *Economics and Free Markets: An Introduction* (Washington, DC: Cato Institute, 2017).

The dead hand and its adverse effects on future digitalpreneurs are emerging. As it emerges, we must consider the short-run and long-run consequences of disincentivizing people from voluntarily exchanging their private resources using e-commerce platforms. If the dead hand takes hold of the emerging entrepreneurial class, what kind of market remains for people to earn, save, and reinvest their savings to enter the economic process? What are the long-run consequences of alternative market decisions for entrepreneurs and their freedom to prosper using their knowledge and personal property? The acquisition and disposition of private property suggest that human action leans toward future aims to substitute less satisfactory circumstances with more satisfactory circumstances. Technological advancements and higher living standards are likely to produce self-expressive market activities geared toward creating better prospects for one's future.

In the short run, will market-space barriers remain low over time for absorption of newcomer entry, or will the barriers to entry to e-commerce rise and increase the costs of doing good business outside the bounds of the average person's capital investment? We may not find answers to the immediate effects the dead hand will have on digitalpreneurs, but in the long run, its effects will become apparent if the incentive to use the digital hand ensures increasing significant gains rather than losses. It is what Bernard Mandeville, the eighteenth-century philosopher, meant when he wrote in his famous exposition *Fable of the Bees*, "It is not insight but restraints imposed upon men by the institutions and traditions of society which make their actions appear rational." [47] Restraints of time and place, and the artificiality of consumer choice, are the effects of entrepreneurial plans that are the causes of the diverting of human action toward the digital hand. Will the dead hand prevail? Is the market space the final free-market frontier?

---

[47] . B. Mandeville, *The Fable of the Bees; or, Private Vices, Public Benefits* (Indianapolis, IN: Liberty Fund, 1806).

Conclusion

The ideas presented in the preceding chapters explain the reasons why entrepreneurship does not have a set narrative about who can and who cannot participate in the marketplace in the entrepreneur function. As the previous chapters in this book elucidated, there is an embedded culture of entrepreneurship within society and between societies. The notion of a culture of entrepreneurship within a societal framework gets to a fundamental idea that there is an enterprising nature among people in society that is embedded in the institutions of entrepreneurship that affects the marketplace and, because of the economic system, causes shifts and changes that are in many ways beneficial to an entrepreneurial society. In fact, the entrepreneur plays a vital role in the function of a marketplace because the entrepreneur, among other things, has no counterpart when it comes to economic and individual development. That is, entrepreneurs do not have to be entertainers or big names in the media; they are (and can be) you, your neighbor, and my neighbor—anyone seeking to use their resources and property as a means to serve someone else via the marketplace.

A culture of entrepreneurship sets a stage for many to

think of themselves as part of a larger culture that embraces innovation, invention, and change in products and services that, in the end, help everyone achieve their goals. The cultural aspects of entrepreneurship reside in the institutions of entrepreneurship that have yet to be altered by human design. Values, rituals, language, family, money, and markets are intercorrelated with the institutions of entrepreneurship. The problem uncovered in this book is that it is easy for society to drift away from the positive attitudes that give rise to entrepreneurial energy because of the thinking that "it [a new invention] has already been done." [48]

There are places in cities and towns that encompass people engaging in buying and selling services. There are people in areas of the world who develop and create art that people might enjoy. There are people online reaping the benefits of technology; the good technology allows for their music to spread widely and make a profit or a loss. There are cities and regions with entrepreneurial enclaves of various ethnic and social affiliations, where goods and services are exchanged with other or similar peoples. That is how entrepreneurship has been typically viewed from the vantage point of real people. Moreover, in other contexts, people who have lost employment became displaced entrepreneurs, forced to enter the market using their capital and knowledge instead of their corporate jobs.

We cannot doubt that regional aspects of a culture contribute to the increased or decreased amount of entrepreneurship globally. Spontaneous entrepreneurial marketplaces lend themselves to more significant

---

[48] . J. Schumpeter, *The Economics and Sociology of Capitalism* (Princeton, NJ: Princeton University Press, 1991).

entrepreneurship in all its forms. People and regions vary; therefore, the reactions due to circumstances and marketplaces must also vary. Variation of responses to market changes should not be surprising because the market itself is a mechanism that allocates and reallocates scarce resources. A culture of entrepreneurship understands that decisions and situations are not unique in and of themselves. It is the situation that creates unique decisions.

Entrepreneurs like to act first, employing capital or using productive heterogeneous resources with the complement of labor, as they enter markets before competitors. Resources are not finite, and neither is time. Entrepreneurial types can be characteristically categorized as initiative-takers and independent thinkers; Aristotle called them *prime movers*. How entrepreneurs think of and use time is different from non-entrepreneurs.

The entrepreneur's subjective valuation of time and use of resources for future improvement signifies their inherent high time preference. The entrepreneur wants to act sooner rather than later on profit opportunities. There is a difference between consumer time preference and the entrepreneur's time preference and the subjective marginal utility of future and present pursuits and investments. Better yet, what is the consequence of capital and entrepreneurial use of their capital over time? The impossibility of perfect timing of resource uses and market changes can be attributed to the fact that entrepreneurship is in many ways shifting toward the accordance of the passage of time, which depends on the durability and nondurability of the goods at the entrepreneur's disposal. We can look at it this way:

Often we stroll in the streets of an ancient town, the merchants' palaces turned into hotels, the former stables now garages, and the old warehouses which have become modern workshops, remind us of the impossibility of planning for the remote future. [49]

These broad factors are cultivated by the structure of a continuous and relentless entrepreneurial force, culture, or class, which Joseph Schumpeter referenced as a distinguishable "shared social *a priori.*" [50] Some people start their careers as entrepreneurs, and some end their careers as entrepreneurs. This is the transition of life that cannot be seen on the surface of the inner workings of society; it is the economic system shifting the circumstances that dictate whether entrepreneurial pursuits are advantageous. Some do not intend to become an entrepreneur for a long period, while others live the entrepreneurial lifestyle.

Humans possess extensive variations, not only in a cultural sense but of skills, ideas, and purposes. How, then, are these variations in abilities and pursuits going to flourish in any other economic system than one that allows individuals to put their best foot forward on their own accord? An economic system provides individuals more than one chance at any given calling or pursuit that an individual may have at a particular point in life. What kind of economic

---

[49] . L. Lachmann, *Capital and Its Structure* (Auburn, AL: The Ludwig von Mises Institute, 2007).

[50] . J. A. Schumpeter, *The Economics and Sociology of Capitalism* (Princeton, NJ: Princeton University Press, 1991).

system is arranged to change industries, marketplaces, or careers any time they feel there is something better on the horizon? The mere fact that people feel that the horizon is greener on the other side is based on their faith in the guidance of institutions. Entrepreneurial institutions leading to entrepreneurial paths should not be deliberately designed and articulated; instead, they must be structured by the known rules experienced in the marketplace order. Everyone in this entrepreneurial culture is linked to one another and is communicating through the actions of one another. Institutions of entrepreneurship serving as a guidepost, if you will, of institutions involving entrepreneurship set forth a culture where a vast number of people can do things that are altogether different from what is or is not "preordained to the individual." [51] A culture of entrepreneurship is a way out of the rut of outmoded conventions, as Schumpeter said. This is only part of the issue outlined in this book. The other aspect of institutions as a signpost is the ever predictable nature of institutional shifts.

Shifts in market circumstances that alert entrepreneurs to how to shape their plans, discoveries, and use of resources "enable each of us to rely on the actions of thousands of anonymous others about whose individual purposes and plans we can know nothing." [52] Is the culture of entrepreneurship akin to a constellation of moving parts of the whole or a force that once in motion tends to stay in motion? To put it another way, whether entrepreneurship takes place in the last free-market frontier—e-commerce—more people will

---

[51] . Schumpeter, *The Economics and Sociology of Capitalism*.
[52] . M. L. Lachmann, *The Legacy of Max Weber* (Berkeley, CA: Glendessary Press, 1971).

gravitate to the entrepreneurial format and environment that is conducive to produce and sell their products or services to bring a return on their investment. Once the motion has started, it typically stays in motion—more entrepreneurs will produce more entrepreneurs, thereby causing a new climate that cultivates the risks involved in the production and offering of wants and needs for human flourishing.

Most of the market activities in which entrepreneurs are engaged are readily seen as a product or a service offering—some in the form of business capital equipment. The seen activities via products and services allow consumers to buy and sell things or provide services at locations to customers. If we examine the unseen activities that emerge via the marketplace, we can observe how entrepreneurship perpetuates the market process—that is, discovery.

History, heroes, industries, and marketplaces have been established by those who came before us. They will also work well for those who come after us. Therefore, it is the entrepreneurs themselves who are the cause of entrepreneurship. Culture is linked to the action of entrepreneurship and the effect it has on society. The real world shows no distinction between those who make the new or reproduce the tried and true, those who want to do more for themselves and serve others in the marketplace. As long as consumers seek value in products or services and use them intentionally and unintentionally for purposes unknown beforehand, and as long as entrepreneurs serve consumers by applying their own resources and tacit knowledge to profit mentally or in exchange, in accordance with the rule of the market order of the *komos*, the entrepreneurial culture will persist.

*The human person is at the heart of the
economy, culture, and ethics.*

Persona humana in corde est oeconomiae, culturae et ethicae.

Printed in the United States
by Baker & Taylor Publisher Services